ANY WAY OUT

Also by Ann Vitorovich: *Whom Shall I Fear* **To order, call 1-800-765-6955.**
Visit us at **www.reviewandherald.com** for information on other
Review and Herald® products.

ANY WAY

*Twin brothers. Two paths.
No chance.*

ANN VITOROVICH

REVIEW AND HERALD® PUBLISHING ASSOCIATION

Since 1861 | www.reviewandherald.com

Review and Herald® titles may be purchased in bulk for educational, business, fund-raising, or sales promotional use. For information, please e-mail SpecialMarkets@reviewandherald.com.

The Review and Herald® Publishing Association publishes biblically-based materials for spiritual, physical, and mental growth and Christian discipleship.

The author assumes full responsibility for the accuracy of all facts and quotations as cited in this book. Some of the names have been changed to protect their privacy.

Texts credited to NIV are from the *Holy Bible, New International Version.* Copyright © 1973, 1978, 1984, International Bible Society. Used by permission of Zondervan Bible Publishers.

This book was
Edited by JoAlyce Waugh
Copyedited by Kathy Pepper
Cover Designed by Trent Truman
Interior Designed by Tina M. Ivany
Cover art by © iStockphoto.com / yarche / ranplett / NeilLang / JordiDelgado
Typeset:Bembo 11/14

PRINTED IN U.S.A.

14 13 12 11 10   5 4 3 2 1

Library of Congress Cataloging-in-Publication Data

Vitorovich, Ann, 1933–
  Any way out : twin brothers, two paths, no chance / Ann Vitorovich.
       p. cm.
  Includes bibliographical references and index.
  ISBN 978-0-8280-2338-2 (alk. paper)
  1. Vitorovic, Voja. 2. Vitorovic, Cveja. 3. Twins--Biography. 4. Defectors--Yugoslavia--Biography. 5. Serbs--Yugoslavia--Biography. 6. Seventh-Day Adventists--Biography. 7. Yugoslavia--Biography. I. Title.
  CT1458.V56V58 2009
  949.702092--dc22
  [B]

                                    2009023004

ISBN 978-0-8280-2338-2

DEDICATION

To my husband, Voya,
my mate and companion for the past 50 years,
whose stories have inspired my writing,
and who came a long way to find me.

Also to my brother-in-law, Steve,
who has been such an important part of both our lives.

DICTIONARY

Word	Meaning	Language
Altersheim	senior residence	German
Architekt	architect	German
autoput	highway	Serbian
autostrada	highway	Italian
benvenuti in Italia	welcome to Italy	Italian
burazeru	brother (slang)	Serbian
bruder	brother	German
carabinieri	policemen	Italian
certainment	certainly	French
Come si chiama	What's the name?	Italian
Dragi Mladen i Mela	Dear Mladen and Mela	Serbian
Fluchtlinge Lager	refugee camp	German
gelato	Italian ice cream	Italian
Gendarmerie/Polizei	police	French/German
guten morgen	good morning	German
herr	sir	German
Jugoslavija	Yugoslavia	Serbian
Kafana Dubrovnik	Café Dubrovnik	Serbian
karaula	guard house	Serbian
komision	consignment shop	Serbian
kume or kum	best man (according to usage in sentence)	Serbian
la langue Français	the French language	French
Österreich	Austria	German
passare la dogana	to go through customs	Italian
pastisseries	bakery	French
pensione	guest-house	Italian
podvarak	cabbage dish with smoked beef	Serbian
pop	priest	Serbian
quanto	How much?	Italian
signore	sir	Italian
soggiorno	sojourn	Italian
trattoria	local eatery	Italian
tromedja	the point where the borders of three countries meet	Serbian
unglaublich	unbelievable	German
vedete	see	Italian
Viva il Papa!	Long live the Pope!	Italian
Volksdeutscher	a person of German descent born in Yugoslavia	German
willkommen	welcome	German

CONTENTS

CHAPTER 1

THE GRAY FALCON AND THE PROMISE

Voja (VOH-ya) peered into the dusty display window of the Putnik Travel Agency and caught his breath. He squinted, brushed his coat sleeve across the window to wipe away the streaks made by melting snow, and looked again. There it was in the center of the display—the list he had waited for, obsessed over, fantasized about, and lived and breathed for, for the past six weeks. Yet faced with it now, he trembled and turned away.

Glancing across the street, he drew a deep breath, blew it out slowly, and turned back to the window. "Tourist Group to Rome, May 13 to 22, 1957," the poster caption read. Beneath the caption were two columns of names: A . . . B . . . V . . . , he anxiously scanned the names listed in Cyrillic alphabetical order. Five lines down, he stopped abruptly and gasped when he saw it: *Vitorovic, Vojislav*—his full name.

A laugh surged up from his belly. He wanted to cheer or shout, but the sounds of approaching footsteps and muffled conversation squelched his exuberance and the laughter slid down his throat in a great big gulp. Suddenly he was giddy with excitement. *This is my ticket to freedom!* he exulted as he turned quickly and hurried away.

Now his destination was Kalemegdan Park, a charming oasis in the center of Belgrade. Sitting like a queen on a limestone throne, the massive blue-red brick walls of an ancient Turkish fortress sprawled across the crest of the promontory overlooking the convergence of the Sava and Danube rivers. Massive stone walls gracefully terraced the steep hill. There on the top terrace, Voja found his identical twin brother, Cveja (TSVE-ya) and drew him to a secluded bench.

The two men, dressed alike in long, gray, wool Cromby coats, sat facing each other, a slight wind ruffling their wavy chestnut-brown hair. Voja's words tumbled out like a flood. "I'm going to Rome. It's official. I just came from Putnik!" He grinned roguishly at Cveja, whose mouth hung open in surprise.

"You're not serious! I can't believe it," Cveja managed at last.

"I know, I know! I can't believe it myself," Voja rejoiced. "They posted the list today. When I spotted my name as the assistant tour guide, I nearly jumped out of my skin." He gestured wildly with his hands. "Fifteen hundred people applied. Would you believe, only 50 were approved!" He shook his head, irritated by the word "approved."

The two men stared at each other for a few moments. Then Cveja chuckled. "You must have given the UDBA *some* interview! Apparenly, you impressed them with your knowledge. Or was it your irresistible charm?" He tilted his head to the side, a mischevious grin playing at the corners of his mouth.

"Charm?" Voja tossed his head back and laughed. "The secret police are not known for being susceptible. As for the interview, it was more like an interrogation. The uniformed colonel hurled questions, and the civilian recorded my answers. After seven semesters studying the history of art and architecture, Rome is engraved on my mind—so that part was easy."

Cveja's lighthearted manner suddenly turned serious, his voice subdued. "They must expect you to return."

The twins stopped talking and sat back as if taking in the view when a young couple walking hand in hand approached. The sun had finally come out after the most recent frigid spell, and many of the city residents were enjoying the mid-January day outdoors. The couple passed, and the twins resumed their conversation.

"Evidently. We do have that September appointment with the military," Voja replied. He leaned forward. "That's one of the reasons I didn't expect to be selected."

"What about Mica [MEE-cha]?" Cveja asked. "A brother-in-law who just got out of political prison couldn't have enhanced your credentials."

Voja nodded. "Having a dissident in the family is bad enough, but not one Communist Party member to show isn't exactly a good recommendation, either." He shrugged slightly. "Strange how they ignored those facts."

After a long pause, Cveja said slowly, "For years we've dreamed of going to America. Now that it seems within our reach, it feels a little scary." He leaned toward his brother and cleared his throat. "I never thought your scheme would work."

"It hasn't yet," Voja answered quickly. "This trip will get me out of the country. I still have to defect, and you need to escape." His face suddenly became troubled. "That's what worries me, Cveja—how you'll escape."

Escape. It was an eventuality to which Cveja had not given much serious thought. He took a deep breath, pushed out his chest, and straightened his back, meanwhile shifting his trousers with his forearms so that the seams went crooked—a nervous habit he had acquired. "Not to worry, Brother," he said confidently, "you know how persistent I can be. All I need is a guide who can take me across the border, someone I can trust."

"Sure. Some of our friends left that way," Voya said and looked away. "But what about those who disappeared, the ones we never heard from?" He turned his head and locked eyes with his brother, a sharp pain stabbing through his chest. "I don't know, Cveja. What if one of us doesn't make it?"

The unanswered question hung heavily in the air. Oblivious to the brothers' plight, pigeons cooed and darted across the concrete walk in front of the bench. Suddenly taking flight, the birds swooped down to the river, and then soared into the sky again. Here on this historic site—an ever-present reminder of the continuing struggle of the Serbs against foreign invaders and occupiers—the twins grappled with their own quest for freedom. Situated as Yugoslavia was in the Balkans at the juncture of East and West, on the fault line between Byzantium and Rome, their people were vulnerable to every conquering army that passed through. Now another alien occupier oppressed them—atheistic Communism.

Cveja broke the tension, his voice light again. "Remember, Brother, you're the trail blazer! You came into this world first. You never did let me forget that 10-minute difference." He laughed. "It's only right that you forge ahead."

They had been through all this before, back when Voja first told Cveja about the poster advertising the trip and the assistant tour guide position. The main guide would be a Communist, of course. Cveja had agreed to remain behind as surety so Voja could apply. The authorities would never grant passports to both brothers. Cveja let Voja chance the easier route, a sacrifice not lost on Voja. As the younger twin, Cveja often deferred to him, although of the two, Cveja had more determination and drive. He would persevere when Voja might give up. This knowledge about his brother gave Voja comfort. Still he wrestled with immense feelings of guilt. He was deserting his twin, leaving him behind. They had never been separated before, and his heart ached already.

"You have until September 22," Voja reminded his brother, a hint of urgency in his voice. "If the reports are true, the United States intends to cut off immigration from Communist countries when Eisenhower leaves office. We would have to complete the immigration process before then, and with quotas opening and closing, we have no idea how long that will take." The intensity in his voice heightened. "But if you don't escape before going into the army, it will be too late when you get out. America will not be open to Yugoslavs anymore."

"Eight months. Time enough," Cveja said too confidently, but Voja still felt reassured. "Remember, your trip to Rome won't exactly be a joy ride." Cveja turned the focus back onto his brother. "Spies will infiltrate your group, pretending to be tourists. Someone will be watching your every move."

Simultaneously drawing a deep breath, the two men stood up and strolled to the black iron railing. Dense strands of green and brown ivy hung like living curtains from the rail down to the ramparts beneath. Leaning over the rail they listened to the sound of rushing waters below, the gray Sava surging into the dark-blue Danube, which was dappled with chunks of ice. Beyond the convergence of the two rivers, international freighters navigated the water highway through Central Europe to the Black Sea. The irony was not lost on the brothers—those nearby ships sailed freely, without restrictive borders or boundaries.

"Remember that promise in Jeremiah 29:11?" Voja asked. He repeated it in part, "'For I know the plans I have for you . . . plans to give you hope and a future.'" Turning around, he leaned back against the railing. "I read that verse this morning. And when I saw my name on the list, it really hit me." His throat tightened, and his eyes misted over. "It seemed like God was opening the door, as if He was saying, 'Here's your chance.' It gave me such joy!"

Cveja turned to face the city skyline, and Voja followed his gaze to the gilded tower of Belgrade's Orthodox Cathedral of St. Michael the Archangel in the distance. Many times they had viewed the headless, shrunken body of Czar Lazar which had been preserved in a glass sarcophagus. The last king of the medieval Kingdom of Serbia, which had flourished for 200 years, Czar Lazar was beheaded by the Ottoman Turks at the Battle of Kosovo in 1389. This defeat plunged the Serbian Kingdom into 500 years of subjection to Ottoman Turkish rule.

"Czar Lazar wasn't deterred by overwhelming odds," Cveja mused. "His small army stood against the Islamic invaders to defend his people's freedom, land, and Orthodox Christian faith." His voice grew stronger and more confident. "It's our heritage to seek freedom."

The moist river air rose up the bluff while the two men stood contemplating their futures. The thick, dank scent filtered into their lungs and settled into their memory. Like the lore of the land that spawned them and the culture that shaped them, they would carry the memory of that scent wherever they went.

As the twins strolled along the walkway, the wind picked up. Pausing at the foot of the towering Messenger of Victory memorial, their eyes traveled up its fluted, white-marble pedestal to the bronze statue on top. The nude man stood with his back to the park, his face looking out over the rivers toward the open plain beyond—the plain from which most invasions of their country had come. In his outstretched hand he held a bronze falcon.

"*Sivi Soko* [Gray falcon]," Cveja said thoughtfully. It was the name given to the brave and courageous, the symbol of good fortune in Serbian mythology. Cveja's eyes rested on the bird, but his thoughts ran ahead. "Look at his wings. He's ready to fly."

As the sun began to fade on the horizon and shadows on the hillside lengthened, Voja glanced at his watch. "We'd better hurry, or we'll miss the trolley bus," he said. With new vigor in their steps, the twins hurried out of the park. The idea of freedom, set to music in their people's ancient, haunting ballads, now burned bright in their hearts, shouted in their minds, and filled them with secret joy.

While they waited at the trolley bus stop, Voja pointed to the sky. The clouds had parted and a bird appeared, gliding gracefully on the wind and circling high above their heads. The twins exchanged glances and then watched it fly through the endless sky, reveling in its freedom until the bird vanished from sight. *Was that a gray falcon?* Voja wondered. Before long the last trolley bus on their route home arrived, and the twins climbed aboard.

Home was a three-room flat situated at the rear of an L-shaped, yellow-stuccoed building accessed through a gated courtyard, but Voja hesitated at the door. All the way there he had worried about how to break the news to the rest of his family. They knew he had applied for the trip but, like Cveja, did not expect him to be selected.

"My brothers!" their sister Nata (NAH-ta) bubbled joyfully as they entered. Turning from the cast-iron, wood-fueled cookstove that also heated the apartment, she wiped her hands quickly on a white linen dish towel, and then rushed to take their coats.

"We're ready to eat if you are," she announced, returning from the other room. As she transfered a pan of stuffed peppers to the table, the savory aroma wafted through the air. She ladled a portion onto a plate for their mother, Mara (MAH-ra), who sat at a small table closer to the stove so she could keep warm. Then she joined her husband, Mica, and her brothers at the kitchen table.

All through dinner the family chattered and laughed. But tonight, Voja's usual enthusiasm and wit seemed restrained. Half-listening to the conversation, he unconsciously traced with his finger the word "Rome" on the table-cloth and on his pant leg.

As he watched the family interact, Voja noticed as if for the first time how easily laughter flowed in the family. Mother's laugh was relaxed and husky, like her speaking voice. Nata sputtered into a laugh, like a faucet suddenly turned on after the water supply had been shut off. Cveja laughed as if trying to smother his mirth, with his hand to his mouth like Nata. Mi a's laughter was robust and infectious.

The conversation whirled around him as Voja tried to recall the laughter of his sisters Vera (VEH-ra) and Leka (LEH-ka), both of whom had married and moved to other towns. Vera gurgled when she laughed, like water bubbling up from a spring. When she ran out of breath, she'd take a wheezy gasp of air without pausing and continue to laugh and talk simultaneously. Leka, their half-sister and eldest sibling, laughed a lot like Vera, giggling and gesturing animatedly all at once. Anyone listening to the sisters' laughter could tell they were related. He tried to recall his father's laughter which had been silenced by death six years before. Yes, Ilija's (EE-lee-ya's) easy laughter had been deep and hearty and, like Vera, he tended to talk and laugh all at the same time.

"What's wrong, Voja? You've hardly touched your food." Nata's query interrupted his thoughts. She stood over him with the platter of peppers and frowned at the half-eaten portion on his plate. "Here, take another one." She bent over and ladled another portion onto his plate, spooning tomato sauce over it before he could protest. To Nata, no one ever ate enough. She was always serving, always smiling. But he knew she reserved a special glow of pride and affection for her twin brothers.

"Brrmm, brrmm." Noises from the corner drew Voja's attention to two-year-old Jovica (YOH-vee-tsa) who knelt on a pillow in the corner pushing around a red wooden car. He lifted it in the air and flew it in a circle, glancing over to see if anyone was watching.

"Čita Majmun [CHEE-ta MY-moon, (Cheeta, the Chimp)]!" Voja exclaimed, catching Jovica's eye. The twins had nicknamed their beloved nephew after Tarzan's amusing sidekick when Jovica was just 18 months old. "You're white as cheese!" Voja teased, looking at Jovica's corn-silk colored hair and pale skin. Jovica smiled back shyly, his raised eyebrows and wrinkled forehead blending into a quizzical look that was both endearing and earnest.

Voja remembered Nata's great joy when she became pregnant. Mica's transfer to a Belgrade prison toward the end of his sentence had allowed him to participate in a prison-work program in which he painted the houses of high-ranking Communist Party members. Under minimal supervision en route to work sites, he occasionally met secretly with Nata in the twins' rented room.

Sitting back in his chair now, fork in hand, Voja gazed around the room. Mica had painted the apartment and retrieved the couple's furniture from a friend's shed where it had been stored during his seven-and-a-half-year incarceration. Prior to Mica's arrest and their subsequent eviction, the twins had lived with the couple in another apartment when they first moved to Belgrade to study at the university.

After his release just seven months earlier, Mica had learned of the vacancy from his best friend's widow, who lived in the front apartment of the building with her second husband and her son, Grujica (GROO-yee-tsa), a friend of the twins. When the apartment was ready, Nata moved back to Belgrade from the family farm in Glušci where she had lived with her parents since the eviction. Jovica came with her, and since Ilija had died in the interim, Mara boarded up the farmhouse, leased the little land they had left to family members, and moved to Belgrade with Nata. Shortly afterward, the couple invited the twins to join them.

After dinner Nata washed the dishes, covered them with a clean linen dishcloth, and left them to drain on the stainless steel counter. Only then did she return to the cleared table where the others remained seated. Their mother watched from her chair near the stove, her large twinkling blue eyes and sweet smile framed by the dark kerchief covering her hair.

Voja shot a glance at Cveja. Swallowing the lump in his throat, he began, "I went to Putnik today."

Four pairs of eyes stared at him expectantly. Even Jovica looked up. "You remember that I told you about the trip to Rome? Well, the list came out today." Glancing at each face, he wrung his fingers nervously. "My name was on it."

No sooner had the words left Voja's lips than Mica jumped up and wrapped him in a bear hug. "That's great news! Something big is going to happen in this family!" he exclaimed, his dark eyes intense. Returning to the edge of his chair, he leaned forward and shook his index finger at Voja. "You have to be very cautious. No one must find out about your plan."

Voja watched his mother shift her gaze from him to Cveja, and back to him as if she already anticipated losing both sons and wanted to etch their images onto her mind. Looking into her eyes, he saw no tears. Actually he had never once seen her cry. Not when he and his brother left home at age 11 to continue their schooling in another town, and not even when their father died. God was her anchor and strength, and she accepted all things as coming from His hand.

"*Dušo moja, puna ku o moja, neka te Bog blagoslovi* [My soul, my full house, may God bless you]," Mara finally said, her voice low and lilting as she met Voja's steady gaze. She repeated her favorite phrase—words she had said so often throughout the years. "*Sve e pro i a Gospod e do i* [Everything will pass and the Lord will come]."

Nata remained uncharacteristically quiet. A lock of dark curly hair fell over her forehead, and she pushed it back absently. Her slippered feet planted flat on the floor, she sat with her hands folded in her aproned lap, her hazel eyes blinking rapidly as she listened.

Nata will fill the gap after we leave. She'll take care of Mother, Voja told himself, though his heart ached for his sister. He had never forgotten how she worked the farm in place of him and Cveja so that their father would allow them to go to high school. Had it not been for God and Nata, the twins would still be uneducated peasants. Much of their family's farm had been nationalized—their grain mill, brick factory, and saw mill confiscated by the government. Yes, he owed much to Nata. And now that her world had finally come together again, he had brought it crashing down around her. The thought grieved him.

"You know that there's no future for us here. The regime gave us a good education—at least that much—but even that doesn't count if you don't belong to the party," Voja finally said, repeating facts they already knew.

Mica nodded silently in agreement, an inscrutable expression settling on his face. He, more so than any of them, was acquainted with this particular detail—since his release from prison he had been stripped of all civil rights.

"A classless society, equality, and brotherhood are what the Partisans promised," Cveja continued his brother's train of thought. "But when they came to power with Josip Broz Tito as president, the communist leaders formed their own bourgeoisie." He shrugged his shoulders. "Since Tito broke with the Soviets, he's relaxed some restrictions, but the machine is still the same. The individual counts for nothing—just a cog in the wheel of the state. The only good is the good of the state."

"Besides, as Christians, we all know we're second-class citizens," Voja said. "The constitution supposedly allows for religious freedom, but Sabbathkeepers suffer anyway."

Voja referred to the church to which their mother had converted while the twins were still infants. It was a Protestant church considered by the people to be an American religion. Most Serbs belonged to the Serbian Orthodox Church, the national religion. But as Seventh-day Adventists, Mara and her children observed Saturday, the seventh day of the week, the biblical Sabbath. From sunset Friday to sunset Saturday they refrained from secular work and activities.

"Other Christians don't have the problems we have with the six-day work week, since Sunday is a holiday and they go to church on that day," Cveja said. "Our members won't work on Saturday, so they're fined and sometimes fired from jobs. School attendance is another problem."

Most Seventh-day Adventists allowed their minor children to attend classes on Sabbath. The few who didn't suffered the consequences. Among those were their half-sister Leka and her husband, Živan (ZHEE-vahn), who kept their three sons home on Saturday. As a result, they were repeatedly fined. Pera (PEH-rah), Leka's youngest son, had been expelled from several schools—retaliation by the state because his older brother, an excellent student, was pursuing a preaching career.

The conversation lulled when Nata rose from the table, filled a pitcher with water, and took glasses out of the cupboard to arrange on a tray. "You must be thirsty," she said, returning to the table with the tray and pitcher. Then she went back to the stove to warm a glassful of water for her mother.

"Our student deferment expires in September when we turn 27," Cveja said. He cleared his throat. "That's when we're scheduled to report for military service."

"The army should be an interesting experience," Mica chimed in, newly engaged in the conversation. Seventh-day Adventists traditionally avoided involvement in politics, but his political preoccupation and subsequent incarceration had smothered his interest in God and religion. "If you think things are tough now, wait until you tell the army you can't work on Saturday. It's a world of its own."

"So we've heard, so we've heard." Cveja shook his head and looked intently at his brother. "Our friends have told us their horror stories."

Voja nodded in agreement. "God willing, we'll be gone before that." He switched to his favorite subject. "It isn't like this in America. Religion is honored there, and citizens have rights." He flung out his hands. "*Voice of America* broadcasts tell us all about it. In America, even factory workers and housemaids can own cars."

"Oh, but the regime calls that propaganda." Mica cut in with a wry smile, his voice thick with sarcasm. He loved America too.

"But of course," Voja retorted, equally sarcastic. "That's why Americans can come and go as they please and we can't. What kind of government locks its citizens inside their borders? If Communism were a good system, no one would want to leave."

A few weeks later Voja received his passport. Every night before retiring he would flip it open and look at his Italian entry visa. "Monday, May 13—D-Day," he'd mumble to himself, reading the departure date. This became a regular evening ritual.

Employed as an architect by the Seventh-day Adventist Church at their state headquarters in Belgrade, Voja was currently working on plans for a new church in Skopje (SCOPE-yeh), the capital city of the republic of Macedonia. One evening as the twins prepared to retire, he and Cveja discussed the project. "I expect to complete preliminary drawings by April," Voja told him, "but I won't be able to finish the working drawings. Whatever work remains, Cveja, I'm counting on you to complete."

And so early in April, armed with preliminary drawings, Voja met Pastors Anton Lorencin (AHN-tohn LOH-rent-seen) and Radoš Dedi (RAH-dosh DED-eech) there in Belgrade, and they set out by train for Skopje. Eight hours and many stops later they finally arrived. After spending the night in the local pastor's apartment, the four men met the next morning with city zoning and building department officials who approved Voja's plans and authorized him to proceed with the working drawings.

On the return trip to Belgrade, Voja sat with the two pastors, pleased that the meeting had gone well. But as the train rumbled past fields of tobacco and vineyards just beginning to turn green, he argued with himself. *How can I not confide in these men? In one month, I'll be gone. What will they think of me then?* He looked out the window at sheep grazing in a distant field. *Yet if the police question them, they would be in an awkward position if they knew of my plans. However, if they don't know and are questioned, they can truthfully say they know nothing. . . . That's it. I'll keep quiet. Cveja will explain later.*

The days that followed brought warmer weather and the welcome scents of spring. Voja worked feverishly on his project and prepared Cveja to take it over. One day Voja discussed his finances with his mother. "I used most of my savings to pay for the trip. All my expenses are covered while I'm with the group, but when I leave, I'll need some money."

"Go to Mladen's (MLAH-den's) house, to my brother's family," she suggested. "I'm sure they would loan you some gold ducats."

Voja boarded a train bound for his uncle's town the very next day.

"Two ducats won't go far," Mladen's son told Voja after he confided his plan and asked for their help. "Remember, as a refugee in Italy, you may not be allowed to work. Besides, you don't know how long you'll wait. Four ducats would be more realistic. We'll loan you four."

And so, after thanking them and bidding them farewell, Voja left their house with his pockets containing four shiny gold coins engraved with the image of the Austrian Emperor Franz Josef.

On the train back to Belgrade, Voja thought of his last meeting with his friend, also named Mladen, more than a year earlier, just before he left the country. The authorities had granted Mladen a passport to Austria in order to get medical treatment only because he was leaving his wife and two daughters behind. A short time later, when a medical emergency arose, his wife Mela (MEH-la) was allowed to leave also. The two girls remained behind in the care of their grandmother.

Each day during their parents' absence, the girls, Mirjana (MEER-ya-na) and Nevenka (NEH-ven-ka), went to Voja's place after school since he worked from home. At that time Mica was still in prison, and the twins were renting a room from a church member. Every afternoon Voja took the girls to a field full of haystacks where they played and slid down the stacks before taking them to their grandmother. Several months later, through the intervention of the Red Cross, the girls received passports and joined their parents in Austria. Fortunately for the little family, America's immigration quota was open at the time so their papers processed quickly, and they now enjoyed life in New York City.

Voja was full of optimism as he thought of his friends in faraway America and the arrangements which were gradually falling into place for his own trip. And during his last weeks at home, he and Cveja spent every free hour in each other's company. D-day—Monday, May 13—was fast approaching.

In the evenings when the family members gathered around the table, they reminisced and laughed as they talked. Nata had apparently accepted the inevitable and joined in the merriment. *"Sve e pro i a Gospod e do i* [Everything will pass and the Lord will come]," his mother reminded him. No matter what happened, that one thing remained sure.

In May the large rectangle of grass in the courtyard turned green. The twisted, thorny branches in the flowerbed began changing color and sprouted leaves and buds. In the center of the grassy area, two lime-green benches sat waiting to be occupied.

"A rose between two thorns," Voja quipped one balmy Sunday as he and his brother sat on one of those benches, their happy mother sandwiched between them. As they talked and dreamed of better days, squirrels scurried around foraging for food and chasing one another up the lone acacia tree which was by now in full-scented bloom. Little Jovica reveled in the freedom of the out-of-doors, pulling behind him a little wooden truck that clattered on the uneven concrete pavement as he scampered across the length of the courtyard.

The last few days flew by, and finally Monday, May 13, arrived. Late that night, Voja would leave for the train station to meet with the tour group. Nata prepared his favorite foods for dinner: *gibanica* (GHEE-ba-nee-tsa [baked cheese strudel]), *sarma* (SAHR-ma [stuffed cabbage]), and Czech torte for dessert. Gathered around the table for their final meal together, the finality of the situation brought an abrupt cessation to the normally lively table talk. For the past four months, each family member had lived in anticipation of this night, and everything that needed saying had already been said.

Sprawled out on the floor on his stomach, Jovica stacked colorful wooden blocks into a fort and peered up at the group every now and then. Voja traced his name with his finger on the tablecloth and sometimes on his pant leg: *Voja Vitorovic, Vitorovic Voja.*

"My soul, my full house, take another piece of *gibanica*," Nata urged, holding the platter of cheese strudel out to him. "You have a long trip ahead."

"I wish I could take the whole pan with me, Nata," Voja declared as he helped himself to another serving. "I sure will miss your good cooking."

He thought of the verse he had read just that morning: *"So do not fear, for I am with you; do not be dismayed, for I am your God. I will strengthen you and help you; I will uphold you with my righteous right hand"* (Isaiah 41:10, NIV). True, he had many fears: fear of the unknown, fear of failure, fear for his brother and their first separation—but his fears were mixed with incredibly exhilarating excitement and hope.

After dinner, conversation suddenly erupted. All at once there seemed to be much to say and not enough time to say it all. "Are you sure you won't take some food with you?" Nata pleaded. "Let me pack you a sack lunch."

"Thanks, Nata, but with all this good food in my stomach, I won't be hungry for a week. Anyway, most of my meals are included," Voja replied, rubbing his belly.

"Did you take the gold ducats?" Mother asked.

"They're in my pocket." Voja patted his pant leg. "I'll put them in my socks before I leave. They need to be kept hidden."

"What about clothing? Are you sure you packed enough?" Nata eyed the small suitcase near the door.

"I have enough for a while. A small suitcase is easier to handle if . . . *when* I'm able to sneak away," Voja corrected himself in mid-sentence.

"Remember, Voja," Mica declared. "This is just the beginning. I won't stay behind for very long."

Voja checked his watch. It was 9:15 p.m., almost time to leave. He took the ducats out of his pocket, each ducat wrapped in a small swatch of fabric, and then taped them together in pairs so they wouldn't slip when he walked on them. Rolling his socks down, he inserted a packet in each heel and then pulled up his socks. Slipping his feet back into his shoes, he tried to adjust to the uncomfortable sensation of foreign objects under his heels. Then the family stood in a circle holding hands while Mother prayed.

"Heavenly Father," she began.

An enormous lump rose in Voja's throat, and he thought he would choke.

"Please be with my firstborn son. Guide him and protect him. Be with us who remain behind. You alone know the future. May Your will be done. Keep us faithful and grateful. And please, Lord, bring us together again. We pray in Jesus' precious name. Amen."

Tears held back for many days flowed freely now, mingling on the wet faces pressed close for the last time as each person wrapped Voja in a hug. Voja held on to Cveja the longest. When Mother kissed Voja on his forehead, even her usually dry eyes looked moist.

CHAPTER 2

TO THE ETERNAL CITY

Voja's Story

The twins stepped out into the cool night air to meet their friend, Grujica, in the shared courtyard. High overhead, wispy clouds drifted lazily across the velvet sky, briefly veiling the full moon. Yellow shafts of light poured from the window of the front apartment, illuminating the lime-green bench on which Voja and Cveja had sat with their mother just days before. Voja shuddered involuntarily as they passed the window—Grujica's stepfather was a Communist Party member.

"You sure are one lucky guy, Voja," Grujica remarked cheerfully as they walked into the darkened street. The wicket door built into the iron courtyard gate clanged shut behind them. "Now since I can't go with you to Rome, you'll have to give me a full report when you get back!"

"Sure, Grujica," Voja replied. He shot a knowing look at Cveja.

Streetcar No. 2 rumbled to a stop in the center portion of the street reserved for public transportation, and the three men climbed aboard. This line ran all night, and the car was half-full of passengers. On the way to the railroad station, Voja stared through the window at his familiar world, from which he would soon vanish.

As the streetcar made its way down the road, Voja watched the pedestrians walking their dogs or rushing home—while he was leaving the land of his ancestors forever. This ancient soil, these cobbled streets, this sky, this air—all were part of his blood and bone. Every sight, every scent, every sound held meaning for him. Packed away in his small suitcase were not only the few items of clothing he carried but the only life he knew. His familiar world seemed to be unraveling before his eyes, threads falling loose which he must reweave into a new design in a strange country far away. But tonight he had an appointment with destiny.

At last the train station loomed ahead. White globe lampposts flanked the length of the building and cast a soft glow over the street and the travelers hurrying about. The three men walked through an arched entryway into a lobby illuminated by crystal chandeliers suspended from a high coffered ceiling. The station seemed unusually crowded for this hour of night, but then Voja had never gone to the train station this late in the day.

Quivering with excitement, he had to reassure himself that this wasn't a dream—that he was actually on his way now. The three men made their way through the lobby past clusters of travelers milling about, hovering at ticket counters, and waiting on wooden benches. Near the depot entrance, a man stood holding a placard that read "Tourist group to Rome."

"Where is the group?" Voja asked aloud. He introduced himself and learned that the man holding the placard was the tour guide whom he would assist.

"You're the first one I've seen," the tour guide replied cordially. "We're meeting at platform one."

Engines hissing, the idling trains at platforms farther down the line belched steam, but there was no train at platform one, the closest platform to the entrance. Grujica and the twins looked around and waited for the others in the tour group to arrive. People soon began drifting toward them, also looking for a train at platform one.

"Where's the train?" one woman wondered loudly. "The guide told us to go to platform one."

"There must be some mistake," a man suggested. He started down the platform to inquire. Two other men from the group followed him.

Several minutes later they returned. "Our train is way back there," they said, turning back and pointing. "We've been moved to platform 13."

"Platform 13 and today is May 13. Does that sound ominous or what?" one of the travelers joked while walking toward the back of the depot with the rest of the group. "Is anyone superstitious? There may be more surprises in store!" Laughter erupted from his companions, transforming a momentary inconvenience into a common cause of conviviality to launch their trip.

As they arrived at platform 13, Grujica surveyed the tour group. "Man, it looks like you're the youngest of the bunch!" he said in low tones, eyeing with displeasure the mostly post-middle age, portly-looking females. "Where are all the chicks?"

"Ach! I have such rotten luck!" Voja lamented, smiling, though chicks were the last thing on his mind at the moment.

The tour guide arrived, carrying an attaché case and a clipboard in his hand. "My apologies for the confusion," he said. He stooped to set his attaché case on the floor. "There was a last-minute change. Now, may I have your attention?" He introduced himself, pulled out a pen, and began calling out the names on his list, checking them off as the individuals responded. "All fifty accounted for," he reported when finished. He slipped his pen into a jacket pocket and slid the list and clipboard into his attaché case.

"We'll occupy those two cars." He gestured toward the two train cars nearest the group and proceeded with instructions. "The composition includes a dining car which we will use and a sleeping car which we will not use." He pointed down the line to each car as he spoke. "Be sure to stay with the group. Don't go off at any time on your own," he concluded.

Voja, Cveja, and Grujica walked toward the second-class car and stopped at the steps. Voja turned to Cveja, a choking sensation in his throat. This was the last farewell. "God be with you, *Burazeru*," they each said, embracing one last time.

The train whistle blasted a warning call.

"Oh, you guys. You'd think Voja was going to Siberia or something, the way you're carrying on!" Grujica remarked, feigning impatience, for he knew how close the twins were. "Have fun, *kume*," he turned to Voja and embraced him. "See you in 10 days. I'll be waiting here when you get back."

Voja picked up his suitcase, climbed the steps, and disappeared into the train car. He walked past several compartments until he found one that was unoccupied. Each uncomfortable step he took reminded him of the gold ducats hidden in his socks. Inside the compartment he chose a window seat and stowed his suitcase on the luggage rack above his head. Folding his raincoat, he placed it on top of his suitcase and settled into his seat. Although it was night, he could see the platform in the milky-white light. Suddenly, Cveja appeared at the window, squinting and peering into the train car. He had been walking alongside the train, trying to locate his brother. Voja knocked on the glass, eliciting a grin from his brother who waved back.

"All aboard!" the conductor called. After two long whistle blasts the locomotive began to puff steam, lurched forward, and moved slowly down the tracks. Cveja ran alongside the train the length of the platform, and then he disappeared from sight as the train pulled out of the station. Picking up speed, the train rattled away into the night, cinders and thick coal smoke bellowing from the smokestack. Through the window Voja watched the darkened city hurtling past. An unfamiliar empty feeling gnawed at the pit of his stomach, even as his nerves tingled with excitement.

In the meantime, five other tourists from the group had joined him in the compartment. Two men sat beside him on the bench and a man and two women on the bench across from him.

"I'm Voja Vitorovic, from Belgrade." Voja introduced himself to the others. The bespectacled, silver-haired man sitting opposite him introduced his wife and sister-in-law. Two stocky, middle-aged men sitting to his side gave their names and said they were friends who lived in Belgrade. Voja listened carefully to the conversation of the group as it ebbed and flowed, seeking clues to which of these people might be spies. But they rambled on excitedly about the trip and the incredible sights to be seen in Rome.

It was quite late, so after about 45 minutes, the group quieted down, agreed to turn out the dim compartment light, and tried to sleep. Voja reached up for his raincoat, placed it against the cold window as a make-shift pillow, and rested his tired head. It had been a long day. As he dozed off, the train sped noisily toward the Italian border.

The next morning Voja and his compartment mates enjoyed a breakfast of scrambled eggs and toast served piping hot in the dining car.

At noon, the train rumbled into the station at Sezana on the Italian border and hissed to a stop. "We'll be transferring to an Italian train at this station," the tour guide announced as he walked through the two cars. Gathering their belongings, the little group exited the compartment and climbed down from the train. Joined by the others, they walked the short distance to a gate over which hung a large, painted, wooden sign welcoming them to Italy. *"Benvenuti in Italia"* it proclaimed.

One by one the passengers lined up and approached the uniformed Italian customs inspector who poked through their luggage, checked their passports, and then waved them through. On the other side of the sign, in Italy, the group reassembled.

I'm standing on Italian soil! I'm actually in the free world! Voja thought as the incredible awareness dawned that he had crossed the border into the West—and freedom. The feeling was strange and intoxicating. Until now all had gone well, and his heart swelled with gratitude.

Once more the tour guide stood before the assembled group, took out his clipboard, and checked off the names on his list. One woman came up missing. The guide paced back and forth, looking around and calling out her name. "Don't worry. Everything will be okay," he assured the group. "Just stick together and wait here. We can't leave until she's found." He walked away to inquire.

Having nothing better to do, the waiting group began to speculate. "The woman was traveling alone," someone noted. "She was dressed too well and looked suspicious." "Probably a Communist taking a large sum of money out of the country," another imagined. Time dragged on and anxiety increased. "Will we encounter the mafia?" an elderly woman asked nervously. "Are we safe here?" another inquired. They had all heard the state-broadcasted propaganda that crime ran rampant in the West.

An hour passed before the woman finally reappeared, red-faced and rather flustered. She reported that she had been taken to a room and strip searched by a female customs agent. "It was so humiliating and disgraceful," she complained indignantly about her ordeal. "These Italians are up to no good."

With all members accounted for, the tour guide led the group to a shiny, modern, Italian electric train. Inside, instead of compartments, rows of double seats lined each side of the train. It appeared the equivalent of Yugoslav first class. Large windows on either side afforded views from any seat. Voja put his suitcase and coat on the rack above him and sat next to the window, the seat beside him remaining unoccupied.

"Passare la dogana!" A voice shouted in the distance. *"Passare la dogana! Passare la dogana!"* The voice grew louder. A uniformed Italian customs agent entered the car. While the agent checked their passports again and stamped them with the date of entry, Voja thought he was sizing up each passenger. Since illegal drugs were not in common use at that time, Voja assumed the man hoped to sell Italian liras and was estimating how many each person might buy. Instantly, Voja's thoughts flew to the ducats in his socks and the paper U.S. dollars and Yugoslav dinar notes and coins in his pockets.

"Signore, we can exchange your Yugoslav dinars for Italian lira," the

customs agent offered, standing in front of him. A Yugoslav customs official accompanying the Italian agent translated since none of the group spoke Italian. Voja gave the agent 20,000 Yugoslav dinars, expecting to receive 42,000 Italian lire at the official exchange rate at that time. Instead, the man gave him 35,000 liras. *Life in Italy is going to be pretty expensive,* Voja grumbled to himself.

Half an hour later, the train slid out of the station for the last leg of their trip to Rome. The tour guide came by to announce that lunch was being served in the dining car, and they soon left the Alps northwest of Sezana and entered Italy's largest plain. Gradually the landscape changed to gently rolling hills draped with vineyards. Here and there a grove of gnarled olive trees or a row of majestic Mediterranean cypresses adorned isolated clusters of houses. Voja felt a thrill of anticipation as he looked forward to seeing the treasures of Rome in person.

They stopped in Padova and then crossed the steel railroad bridge over the Po River, the longest river in Italy. When Voja's ancestors fled to Serbia from Turkish-occupied Bosnia at the turn of the 18th century, they had crossed the Drina River. Serbia had by then attained some independence from the Turks, and his ancestors longed to be free and live on their own land. Many years later, when Austria retaliated by attacking Serbia after the assassination of the archduke in Bosnia, thus starting World War I, the Austrian army crossed the Sava River, and the ensuing battle raged on farmland owned by the Vitorovics and other families. Twice the Serb army drove the Imperial army off Serb land and across the Sava River. And now Voja was crossing a river on his quest for freedom.

As the train passed through the cities of Bologna and Firenze, Voja enjoyed a window-sized view of Renaissance architecture and medieval hill towns. He sat on the edge of his seat, staring through the windows on both sides of the train, trying to take everything in. Late in the afternoon the train pulled into Rome's Stazione Termini with its beautiful marble interior and distinctive outer facade. At long last they had reached the Eternal City—the city that sat on seven hills, where popes and emperors ruled, and where Christians had once been fed to the lions.

The passengers disembarked, and the guide herded his group into a large bus waiting at the curb to transport them to their *pensione.* The gray stucco building with a red corrugated tile roof appeared to be more than a century old, possibly converted from a school or monastery, Voja guessed. One by one the yawning, stretching travelers spilled out of the bus and streamed into the building.

A hot spaghetti-and-meatball supper awaited them in the dining room, and the group quickly seated themselves for their first authentic Italian meal. As they struggled to move the long, slippery strands of spaghetti from plate to mouth without dripping tomato sauce on their clothing, people at first gasped, and then laughed at their common dilemma. Someone cleverly suggested this was Italy's ingenious way of avenging itself for losing the Second World War. Every so often someone rushed to the washroom to purge a spot of sauce from their clothing. Returning to the table, they inevitably tied cloth table napkins around their necks as bibs.

After dinner the tour guide made his announcements. "Tomorrow morning breakfast will be served at 7:00 a.m. At 8:00 a.m. we will leave by bus for Pompeii and Naples." The tourists retrieved their luggage and followed the guide in serpentine procession up the marble staircase to the fourth floor.

"We will occupy the entire floor. Single men and women will sleep five to a room. Men have four rooms at this end." He pointed to the corridor on one side of the building. "Women will sleep in five rooms at the other end. Water closets are located between rooms. The two married couples will stay on the third floor where I have a room," he added. As the singles separated and made their way to their rooms, the guide escorted the two couples down the stairs to two small private rooms. Then he staked out his own room nearest the staircase, and they all retired for the night.

Early the next morning a sharp knock on Voja's door awoke him. "*Ustajte! Vreme da se ustane* [Arise! Time to get up]," the guide's voice called loudly from the other side of the door. After a continental breakfast in the dining room, the refreshed and eager group boarded the bus.

Voja found the drive through Rome's early morning traffic both intriguing and terrifying. *They're mad!* he thought as he watched pedestrians and vehicles scurrying about like ants. *They're trying desperately to keep others from cutting them off, but they're all cutting in front of each other!* Horns tooted loudly, hands and arms gestured wildly, and agitated voices shouted through open windows. *It might have been safer at the Yugoslav border!* Voja thought for a moment. Despite the delightful bedlam, their bus driver made it to the *autostrada* without incident.

Italian four-lane highways at that time imposed no speed limits and the bus traveled well over 65 miles per hour, which seemed fast to Voja compared to traffic on the two-lane Yugoslav highways.

Two hours later they arrived in Pompeii, the site of the ancient Roman city destroyed in A.D. 79 by the eruption of Mt. Vesuvius. Fascinated, the tourists viewed a city frozen in time—the petrified ruins of the forum, temples, theaters and private homes, the shapes of human bodies in various positions immortalized in plaster.

Later an hour spent in Naples exposed Voja to one of Italy's infamously charming street vendors, this one hawking Parker pens. *"Vedete!"* the man said enthusiastically. He pointed to the "Made in U.S.A." sign on the pen. Having studied four years of French and two years of Latin, Voja expected to understand some spoken Italian, but the Neopolitan dialect spoken in Naples swallowed ending letters and syllables and made it hard for him to distinguish words.

"Quanto?" Voja asked, gesturing. On the train to Rome the tour guide had given the group a crash course in Italian conversation, and Voja now put it into practice.

"Two thousand lira," the vendor replied in Italian, his cavalier attitude implying that the price was a virtual give-away.

"No, no!" Voja responded, shaking his head and waving his hand as he proceeded on his way. But the man followed him down the street, his price dropping with every step Voja took.

"One thousand lira," he said finally. That was about US$1.60. Parker pens in Yugoslavia sold for three U.S. dollars at the time. *Now that's a good price*, Voja thought smugly. He stopped and made the purchase, pleased to have struck such a bargain on his first day abroad. Proudly, he slipped the American pen into his inside jacket pocket, promptly forgetting about it as he rushed to catch up with the group.

"Tomorrow we'll visit St. Peter's Basilica, the Vatican Museums, and the Sistine Chapel. Our architect, Voja, will assist me," the guide announced on the bus while driving back to the *pensione* at the end of the day.

As he removed his jacket later that night in his room, Voja caught his reflection in the dresser mirror. To his horror he saw a dark-blue stain on his only white shirt. He tore off his shirt and inspected the ugly blemish. It was twice the size of a ducat. Still standing before the mirror, he glanced up to see another stain on his undershirt in the same place as the one on his dress shirt. He snatched up his jacket to inspect it. On the inside lining, a dark-blue blotch spread across the lower portion of the inside pocket where he had put his "Made in the U.S.A." Parker pen. Yanking out the pen, he glowered at it accusingly. Even as he did so, ink leaked onto his fingers, adding insult to injury. Devastated, Voja went to the tour guide's room to complain.

"I see they got you already," the guide laughed. "Italian factories manufacture copies of famous brand products and sell them as authentics. You should be more careful," he advised.

"I should be more careful," Voja muttered to himself as he left the room. "Easy for him to say." Having brought along only one other change of clothing, Voja found no humor in his predicament.

Early the next morning he awoke to the deep-tones of the church bells that rang on the hour every hour throughout the day. Over breakfast he talked with the tour guide about the day's plans and suggested they divide the group in two. It would be difficult for fifty people to hear one person talking since they would be around other large groups.

It was a glorious morning, and the city awoke to noise and bustle. Shopkeepers whistled and sang as they opened their stores, swept the sidewalk, and pulled down their awnings. Up ahead a woman leaned out of her window to shake out a rug. St. Peter's Basilica in Vatican City was only a short distance from the *pensione*, so both groups decided to walk. When they reached the oval Piazza twenty minutes later, the tour buses were fast arriving, their passengers spilling out and spreading across the plaza like swarms of ants.

Standing in front of the Basilica now, Voja thought of the story of Prince Njegoš (NYEH-gōsh), bishop and leader of the country of Montenegro, visiting Rome in the nineteenth century. When presented with the sacred chain supposed to have bound St. Peter in a Jerusalem dungeon, the other tourists fell to their knees with their arms crossed and reverently kissed the chains. Njegoš looked at the monk who held it, took it in his hands to see its length, and observed, "They really chained him well." Then he returned the chain. Barely able to speak, the stunned monk finally managed, "Will your highness not kiss the chain?" To which Njegoš, turning to leave, replied, "Montenegrins don't kiss chains."

The guide's voice broke into his thoughts. "Lunch will be on your own. Keep together in groups. We'll meet for supper back at the *pensione* at 7:00 p.m.," he announced before they separated. While Voja's group of twenty-five tourists would go through St. Peter's Basilica, the guide would lead his group to the Sistine Chapel.

Voja made a sweeping gesture with his hands and led his group through the sprawling plaza. "The Piazza's impressive Doric colonnade was designed by Giovanni Lorenzo Bernini," he began. "St. Peter's Basilica is the largest church in Christianity and is located in the smallest country in the world, the Vatican. It's also the largest and most important building of the Renaissance. Plans began in 1506. Several architects in succession worked on it until Michelangelo was appointed in 1546."

Upon entering the marvelous church, the awestruck group gasped and gazed around, not knowing where to look first. Their first sensation was of the unexpected chill that permeated the huge building. Through the misty beams of light filling the sanctuary, they marveled at its magnificence and the immensity of its size—people standing at the far end of the broad aisle looked as small as insects.

"The building is approximately 730 feet long and 500 feet wide. At the dome it is 452 feet from the floor to the tip of the lantern," Voja explained. "The sale of indulgences largely financed its construction—and also contributed to Martin Luther's disenchantment with Rome. And, of course, that led to the Protestant Reformation."

Standing beside Michelangelo's Pieta, he told the group, "This is the Madonna della Febre, one of four Pietas sculpted by Michelangelo. But this is the only one he completed. It's also his only work bearing his complete signature."

And so the enchanted group continued the tour, viewed the figure of St. Peter—said to have earlier represented the pagan god Jupiter—and at every juncture oohed and aahed and whispered.

"Where is the closest *trattoria?*" one of them asked sometime near noon.

Not finding one nearby, they bought drinks and *gelato* from a street vendor, and then turned toward the Musei Vaticano and the Sistine Chapel, taking care not to get separated.

"You are looking at the largest uninterrupted fresco in Rome," Voja declared as they stood before the magnificent Last Judgment scene in the Sistine Chapel. "Michelangelo did not allow anyone to see it until he finished it. Not even Pope Paul III. At its unveiling, the pope was overawed. But his master of ceremony objected to the nude figures in the church of God, as did the common people when they saw them. During the following 200 years, subsequent popes commissioned artists to drape them."

From there the group went to the Vatican Palace, and then to the Pantheon with its great dome under which Raffaello Sanzio was buried.

Knowing his time with the group was limited, Voja wanted to squeeze in as many sights as possible. He took out his map of Rome to find the way to Fontana di Trevi. There, with their backs to the huge, elaborate fountain, each person made a wish and threw in a coin. Instead of the traditional wish to return to Rome and the fountain, Voja wished for success in leaving it and for the safety of his brother.

It was late afternoon when they reached the Spanish Steps, the declining sun casting long shadows down the curved stone stairway. On the top steps, still illuminated by the fading light, a wedding party posed for photographs.

On the way back to the *pensione*, Voja ignored the babbling voices of the group and reviewed his plan in his mind—he would be making his move the next day. Soon after discovering his name on the Putnik list, he had written to a married couple, Elizabeth and Djordje (JOR-jeh), childhood friends who had earlier escaped from Zagreb and were now waiting in Rome to immigrate to the United States. A mutual friend had given him their address. Voja had written them again a week before leaving Yugoslavia stating that he would try to slip away on Friday, May 17, a date he had selected arbitrarily. He had asked them to meet him between 10:00 a.m. and noon on the south side of the Piazza San Pietro—St. Peter's Square.

When Voja's group arrived back at the *pensione*, the other group had already begun to eat, and the late arrivals quickly joined them for another pasta meal.

"Since everyone appears to be exhausted, we'll modify tomorrow's plan," the tour guide announced while the bibbed group finished their meal—by now most had found the cure for splattering sauce stains. "Tomorrow morning you'll have free time. But please keep to your group. Be back here for lunch by one o'clock. After lunch we'll leave for Tivoli—the fountains are gorgeous. And then we're off to Villa d'Este. Voja will treat us to the architectural point of view."

Voja could hardly believe his ears. The schedule change facilitated his plan beautifully. He could not have arranged it any better had he tried.

"Breakfast will be served between 8:00 and 9:15 a.m., so you may sleep late if you wish," the guide concluded.

After dinner some of the travelers lingered in the small lobby, sitting together in little groups to recount the day's impressions and experiences, chattering animatedly and roaring with laughter at some anecdote or incident of the day. Cigarette smoke swirled about them like a thick cloud. Although relaxed, their tongues loosened by the alcoholic drinks that filled their glasses, conversations still remained guarded and impersonal. Acutely aware that spies infiltrated every group, everyone kept up their guard. No one trusted anyone else, and at the end of the day, no one knew anything more about their traveling companions than they did the day before.

Voja did not drink or smoke, so he avoided the lobby and went straight to his room. It was quiet there, and he needed to collect his thoughts and pray. This was his only chance. He must succeed. Everything depended on tomorrow.

The next morning he awoke wet with perspiration. He hadn't slept well. Anxious about the day, he had dreamed of being caught and arrested. A glance out the window revealed a gloomy and dreary day, and the soft snoring coming from the other beds in the room informed him that his roommates were still fast asleep. He arose and tiptoed quietly into the bathroom to shave and shower. By the time he finished, the others were awake.

"What makes *you* so ambitious this morning?" one asked from his bed as Voja dressed.

"I couldn't sleep," he replied. "Dreamed all night of angry frescoes. Besides, I'm hungry as a horse. See you at breakfast."

He started down the four flights of stairs to the lobby, alert for any sign of the guide or anyone else in his group. No one was in sight. He entered the dining room and ate alone. By the time he finished breakfast it was almost

8:45 a.m. On the way back up the stairs, he met his roommates going down. *Great timing!* he congratulated himself. So far everything was proceeding perfectly.

Quickly placing his clothing into his suitcase, he frowned once more at the ink spots, donned his jacket, and picked up his suitcase. Throwing his rain-coat over his arm to conceal his suitcase, he poked his head out the door. The corridor was empty. He stepped out and closed the door quietly behind him.

Clutching the banister for support, he descended the staircase on legs that felt like jelly, and his breathing was shallow and rapid. One flight down, the door to the tour guide's room was still closed, and he held his breath as he tip-toed past. His heart thumped wildly in his chest; his mouth was dry as cotton. He prayed under his breath, "Please, God, don't let anyone come by right now," and then wobbled down the next flight of stairs to the first floor landing.

From the top of the wide marble staircase, he could see the lobby on the ground floor. There was no one in sight although the dining room door was still open. On the other side of the lobby near the entrance, a plump woman stood at a desk behind a glass window with her back toward him. This was his chance. He took a deep breath and flew down the remaining stairs. Then he bolted across the marble floor toward the front doors.

CHAPTER 3

A REFUGEE IN ROME

Voja shoved the door open with his free hand, stepped outside, and turned left. His head reeled, and he felt nauseous. No one in the pensione had attempted to stop him. No one had called out. His pulse racing, he dared not look over his shoulder. Hurrying away from the building, he left behind his tour group, the spies that infiltrated it, and the Communist tour guide he had assisted.

The air outside was cool, and a light rain began to sprinkle. Along the street, umbrellas sprouted like colorful mushrooms, hastily opened as people hurried here and there. His raincoat lay draped over his left arm, but he dared not stop to put it on.

It was only a short distance to the corner, and he turned left again. *So far, so good,* he thought. Now that he was out of sight of the *pensione*, no one there could spot him. Breathing a sigh of relief, he eased his pace.

Continuing down the street, he gradually became aware of heavy footfalls squishing on the wet pavement somewhere behind him. He walked faster, but the sound grew louder, the footsteps coming closer. Someone was walking behind him—and gaining ground. The sick feeling in his stomach lurched into his throat.

The recessed entrance of an apartment building appeared ahead, and he quickly ducked into its shadows. Breathless and trembling, he waited. Pressing his body against the cold stone wall, his heart beat wildly in his chest, the perspiration under his damp jacket making his skin crawl. The rain splattered softly on the pavement, and cars swished past on the wet street.

Suddenly the footsteps came to a halt. He stopped breathing and stood motionless, waiting. A few moments later, he peeked out cautiously. A laughing couple, arm in arm under a red umbrella, approached some distance away, but no one stood near him. Whoever had been walking behind him had either stepped into another building or crossed the street. Relieved, he uttered a prayer of thanks as his heart rate and breathing returned to normal and his stomach calmed.

Feeling composed now, he set down his suitcase, swung his raincoat off and shook out the raindrops, and then put his arms into the sleeves and buttoned up the coat. Pulling his collar up around his face, he picked up his suitcase again and stepped into the street. The light drizzle persisted, and he was glad it wasn't any heavier. *The city map, where is it when I need it?* He certainly needed it now, but it was packed away in his suitcase and he couldn't retrieve it. His sense of direction would have to guide him—it had never failed him in the past. But in his present anxious state, his mind went blank, and the narrow, short streets of Old Rome looked alien and strange.

Hurrying on his way, he tried to regain his bearings. He worried whether he was heading in the right direction or not. The last thing he needed was to wind up back at the *pensione*. *What a disaster that would be! Whew!* The thought sliced through him like a cold knife. A glance at his watch showed almost 9:30 a.m. He wondered if his friends had received his letter. Would one of them be waiting? He must arrive before they left. If he didn't get there in time, he would not know how to find their house or get in touch since they had no phone. What would he do then? Where would he spend the night?

The unrelenting drizzle continued to spatter his head and slide down his cheeks. He wandered for what seemed like hours, his mind a jumble of confusion, the streets an inescapable maze. Perspiration dripped from his face along with the rain, and he wiped it away with his hand. At last he spied the Doric colonnades that rimmed St. Peter's Square up ahead. His watch showed 10:30 a.m. By now the rain had eased, and the clouds were beginning to part.

Walking back and forth along the south side of the plaza, he searched the mob of eager tourists for a familiar face. The crowd seemed thinner than when he had been there with the group the day before. Already a sense of isolation in this strange city had begun to seep into his being. He was AWOL—absent without leave—from the tour group, a stranger in an alien country, and about to become Rome's newest refugee.

On the third pass, he spotted them. Ivan's (EE-von's) dark hair stood out above the crowd, and Djordje was with him. Voja's heart leaped with joyful relief. His friends had not let him down.

"Ivan! Djordje!" he called out, waving frantically to attract their attention. Their faces lit up with recognition, and they rushed toward him.

"Brother Serb, you made it after all!" the two men shouted, giving Voja a hearty hug. "We worried you wouldn't get here."

"You guys are undoubtedly the most beautiful sight in Rome! What a relief to these sore eyes!" Voja replied, looking around cautiously. "Let's get out of here. I don't want to run into anyone I know."

"We were so happy to get your letter," Djordje remarked, resting an arm on Voja's shoulder as the three men walked away.

"I was optimistic when I wrote it, but it wasn't until last night that I actually thought I could make it," Voja said. "At the last minute, the tour guide changed the schedule and gave us free time this morning. It was incredible! Otherwise, I might not be here." Voja described what sounded like a coincidence, but in his heart he knew it was God's providence.

Two street cars and a bus ride later, Voja and his friends arrived in Centocelle, a suburb of Rome, where the men were staying. By now the sun shone brightly, and Voja's clothes had dried.

"Brother Serb!" Ivan's sister, Elizabeth, shouted through the open door as she watched them approach. "Welcome to our home away from home!"

"Hey, there's that Šapčanin [(SHOP-cha-neen) a person from Šabac (SHAH-bats)] again!" their mutual friend Željko (ZHEL-yko) said, laughing. He joined Elizabeth at the door.

"We just can't get away from him!" Djordje joked as Elizabeth and Željko welcomed Voja with a hug.

"You have a nice place here. It's fairly new construction," Voja said, surveying the house as he entered.

"Three bedrooms, a kitchen, dining room, all furnished. We share this with two young ladies you know," Elizabeth said. She showed him around and pointed out the various rooms.

"There's room for you, too," Ivan offered. He gestured toward the living room sofa. "You can stay here until you find a place."

"Why don't you park yourself there right now," Elizabeth said. "I'll have lunch on the table in a jiffy, and we can talk while we eat." She smiled and turned toward the kitchen.

Later, as they sat around the table eating and catching up on recent events, Elizabeth confided, "We had to leave our baby behind with Djordje's parents. It was the only way the authorities would allow us to leave." Her voice cracked and tears welled up in her eyes. "That was a year ago. She was just beginning to walk. Now she's probably running around and talking. We've missed all of that."

Djordje gently took her hand and continued the story. "There were 48 of us in the tour group. We were all listed on one collective passport. So when Elizabeth and I defected, we had no documents."

"Have you received political asylum yet?" Voja asked, twirling the spaghetti around his fork like a pro.

"Yes, but we had to wait. It took six months," Djordje replied. "Now we're working with the Red Cross to get our precious daughter out." He looked hopefully at his wife. "When that happens, we'll apply to immigrate to America."

"And you guys?" Voja turned to Ivan and Željko. He paused and leaned back in his chair. "How did you escape?"

"I came with them," Željko replied, nodding toward Djordje and Elizabeth. "We defected from the same tourist group, and we've been together since then."

"I defected from a tourist group a year later," Ivan said. "And of course I found my sister and Djordje here."

"We've been here long enough to learn the ropes," Djordje interjected. "We'll give you some valuable tips. No charge for our expert experience!" he quipped.

The next day was Saturday. While the others took the train to the nearest Adventist church in Rome, Voja remained in the house. His tour group was still in the city, and though unlikely, he couldn't risk running into them.

On Monday Djordje took Voja to Questura di Roma, the police station, to register him as a refugee and apply for *soggiorno*. He needed permission to remain in the country.

"Let me have your passport," Djordje said to Voja as they climbed the steps to enter the building. Djordje handed it to the officer at the desk, who gave Voja some papers to fill out. After Voja completed them, the officer took the documents to the back for review. Several minutes later, the man returned with a paper and Voja's passport in his hand.

"We're issuing you *soggiorno* good for thirty days," the man said in Italian. Djordje translated since he was from a part of Croatia near the Italian border where Italian was also spoken. The officer handed Voja the document. "Keep this with you at all times. It's your identification. Every thirty days as long as you stay here, you must apply for an extension." He paused to be sure his message was understood. "Just remember, you're not allowed to take a job. If you do and we find out, you'll be deported. If we find you lied on your application, you'll be sent back." His voice sounded firm and official. "Come back in a month."

On Tuesday Djordje escorted Voja to the refugee office of the World Council of Churches to apply for political asylum. A tall, good-looking, pleasant-mannered man waited on them.

"Vojislav Vitorovi !" the man intoned, reading his name on the *soggiorno*. "Where are you from?" he asked in fluent Serbian.

"Šabac," Voja replied, since this was the district city of his region. The name of his village would mean nothing to the stranger.

"*Šabačka Čivija* [(SHAH-botch-ka CHEE-vee-ya) Šabac Lynchpins]!" the man announced with a grin. This nickname for the people of Šabac originated long ago from a prank the townspeople once played on their king by removing the lynchpins from the wheels of his royal coach.[*]

Voja smiled. "And you?" he asked.

"I'm from Montenegro. I served in the Yugoslav army. When the Communists took over, I left. Now I live here and work with refugees." He scanned Voja's passport. "I see that your visa is valid until tomorrow. You cannot apply for political asylum until it expires," the man stated. He returned the passport to Voja, who had briefly told him his story.

"I have to warn you, my friend." He leaned forward and lowered his voice. "The Italian *carabinieri* could turn you in. They get paid for every returned refugee, more for educated ones like you." He raised his eyebrows to emphasize his words, then straightened up and extended his hand. "Be careful. I'll see you on Monday."

Voja found a furnished room to share with an Italian fellow in a house a block and a half away from his friends. Some of the Italian liras he had received in trade while with the tour group had gone for postcards and incidentals, and, yes, for his infamous Parker pen, while playing the role of a tourist. The remaining liras were insufficient to pay his first week's rent, so Djordje advanced him enough liras until he could exchange one of his gold ducats at a local bank.

For the rest of the week, Voja kept a low profile. On Monday he returned to the refugee office of the World Council of Churches to apply for political asylum. The same pleasant man accepted his application. "I can't guarantee how long you'll have to wait," he said. "It will take a while to process."

Before writing home Voja waited two weeks to allow things there to calm down. Then addressing the letter to his sister's married name, he used Djordje's name and his Centocelle address for the return. When the Yugoslav authorities censored the incoming mail, they would not find the name Vitorovi anywhere, and Djordje's Croatian name on a letter to Belgrade would not attract attention. He wrote the letter in generic terms and signed it *Brother Voja*.

Lying awake in his room each night, images of home swirled in his mind. His brother's face was constantly before him—their lives were so intertwined. Often when his heart throbbed with loneliness, he talked to him. "Where are you, Cveja? My soul aches each day without word from you. When will you escape? Who will help you? How will you go?" He wondered, too, about his mother and sister. He pictured his mother's smile and imagined Nata's giggly laugh. "Please, Lord, may my family be safe and well," he prayed.

The following Saturday, Voja attended the little Adventist church in Rome for the first time. Upon learning of his refugee status, several friendly church members offered to help him.

"You're an architect. Can you tutor my four boys in math?" one member asked. "I can't pay you, but my wife is a good cook. When you come over, you can stay for dinner."

"You play the guitar?" another member, an attorney, asked. "I've always wanted to learn. Would you teach me? I'll pay you cash."

This help, plus the US$30 that his friends Mladen and Mela sent him each month from New York City, loaned from their limited resources, covered his rent and bought one good meal a day at a nearby *trattoria,* which he supplemented with fresh fruit from small local produce stands. Since arriving in the United States in 1956, his friends' family had grown by two. Mela had been pregnant when they immigrated and gave birth to their third daughter, Nadica (NAH-dee-tsa), two weeks after they arrived in New York City. A son, Djordje, was born eighteen months later.

"I need to buy a light pair of slacks," Voja told Ivan and Djordje one day. "The ones I have are too heavy now that the weather has warmed up."

"We know a store. It's a discount place," they said. "We'll take you there."

When the three men arrived at the store, Voja picked out a nice pair of gray trousers marked 3,500 lira (about six U.S. dollars at that time). It seemed to be a good deal so he made the purchase and returned happily to his room.

A few days later, while eating spaghetti, a drop of tomato sauce fell on his new trousers. He tried to wash out the stain at home, but it wouldn't budge. So he left the slacks soaking in a basin of soapy water. Donning another pair of slacks, he went out again.

Arriving back in his room later, the first thing he did was check on his pants. He reached into the basin to pull them up, and, to his horror, they dissolved into shreds in his hands. Fighting back tears, he gathered the pieces and let them dry out, then put them into a sack and went back to the store. There he showed the owner the remains of his beautiful slacks.

"Don't you know you're not supposed to wash this material?" the man scolded. "It's paper impregnated with cotton." Then he walked off and left Voja standing open-mouthed and stunned, holding the bag and muttering to himself, "Paper pants?" His earlier Parker pen experience came flooding back. "They got me again," he complained.

When Voja visited his friends several days later, Ivan showed him an article in the Italian newspaper. "The Pope is going to make an appearance tomorrow. It's June 29, the Feast of Saints Peter and Paul." He handed Voja the paper. "Thousands of pilgrims will be there. Do you want to go?" he queried as Voja scanned the article.

"Sure, why not?" Voja replied, looking up from the newspaper. "It should be interesting."

The next day the two men stood among thousands of faithful pilgrims crowded into the vast square. *"Viva il Papa! Viva il Papa!"* the crowd cheered and chanted. All eyes focused on the third floor balcony of the Apostolic Palace. When the doors on the balcony edged open, the cheers and chants gave way to gasps. Dressed in white robes, Pope Pius XII appeared like a celestial being, and a hush fell over the crowd. Worshippers stared mute and awed. Then, like a huge wave, the crowd bowed and sank to the ground.

Along with isolated figures scattered throughout the throng, Voja and Ivan remained standing. They waited while the Pope finished blessing the worshippers and went back inside. Many in the crowd were still prostrate when Voja and Ivan turned to go.

"I've never seen anything like this," Voja said as they returned home. "Orthodox Serbs revere their patriarch and priests, but they don't worship them like this. I can't help thinking of when Prince Njegoš's carriage encountered a papal procession on the road to Rome. Even though his Italian coachman begged him to get out of the carriage, Njegoš remained inside, observing the procession through a small window. 'For heaven's sake,' he told the coachman, 'I will not embarrass my small tribe of Montenegrins. Let the pope go his way. Let those get out of their coaches who have done it before. But the Bishop of Montenegro will not.' "

"Historically, the Orthodox Serbs haven't been very compliant with the dictates of Rome, have they?" Ivan laughed.

"I guess not," Voja chuckled. "And Rome hasn't forgotten."

All this time in Rome, Voja had heard nothing about Cveja. Finally, weeks later, a letter from Nata arrived for Voja at Djordje's address. Borrowing an iron from Elizabeth, Voja returned to his room and pressed the letter with the hot iron to bring out any invisible message. In an oppressed society, it was a common practice to write between the lines in lemon juice. The heat of the iron burned the juice and revealed the unseen writing.

He picked up the letter and read, "Cveja has disappeared. We don't know where he is. The UDBA is searching for him. Some people say they saw him. Rumors say he's dead, shot at the border. Mother and I still hold onto faith. We are well, but terribly worried about you both. We love you and pray for you constantly."

"Cveja! Cveja! Oh my brother, Cveja!" Voja cried out in anguish. "Where are you, brother? You must be alive. I can't live if you die. We must meet again." Shaking, he dropped to his knees. "Please God, please bring him out safely," he begged.

A couple of weeks later at church, Voja received quite a surprise. A man he knew from Belgrade was visiting Rome and happened to be in the congregation.

"Have you seen my family? Are they well?" Voja asked him anxiously.

"Yes, I saw your mother and Nata. They're good, but very concerned. Nobody knows where Cveja is. I saw him once in Novi Sad [NO-vee SOD], but he didn't look good. He was running here and there, like a lion in a cage, trying to escape. But that was a while ago."

The awful news plunged Voja into despair. More than three months had elapsed since he had left Yugoslavia. Less than a month remained until the twins were required to report to the army, but still Cveja had not escaped. Returning to his room later, Voja talked to his reflection in the small dresser mirror. It had become his custom whenever the loneliness became unbearable, and tonight he was in agony.

"Oh, *brate moj* [my brother], you must be going through hell. I can feel it in my bones. Please, God, protect him from harm. Help him to find a way out." Weak with grief, he felt it would be his fault if anything happened to his brother.

"The Italian authorities still haven't granted me political asylum," Voja complained to his friends one day as they visited. "I've extended my *soggiorno* three times already. How long does it take? This waiting is making me nervous."

"It will come. You have to be patient. We had to wait too," they explained. "So what have you been up to?" they asked, changing the subject. "We haven't seen much of you lately."

"I'm tutoring some kids and giving private guitar lessons," Voja explained. "It's helping me learn Italian. I point to an object and ask them, '*Come si chiama*' and they tell me the name in Italian. It's really easy. I'm gradually picking up the language."

September finally rolled around, bringing cooler weather. The twins' twenty-eighth birthday on September 9 came and went, uncelebrated. Nata had not written again, and Voja heard no more news about his brother. He had left Belgrade in the spring when the trees were green, and now autumn scents filled the air. The winds would soon blow, the leaves would turn color and fall away, and before long the trees would be bare. Voja thought back to the evening he'd spent with his brother at Kalemegdan Park when the future seemed so promising and bright. "I was so optimistic. It was all a dream," he chastised himself. "Please, God, don't let this turn into a nightmare. I'm scared how it will end."

One day a postcard arrived at Djordje's house addressed to Voja. A phone call from Elizabeth sent Voja flying to their house. The return address on the card was Jennersdorf Refugee Camp in Austria.

"I can't believe my eyes!" Voja exclaimed, the tone of his voice escalating as he eagerly read the card. "It's from Cveja! He escaped! He's OK, and he's in Austria!" He read the message aloud, "My dear brother, Voja. Thanks be to God, I finally crossed the border. In a few days I should receive political asylum. As soon as I do, I'll go to Salzburg and find a job."

Voja felt that he would burst from happiness and relief. "Not only is Cveja alive and well, but he's safe in Austria! He's really safe!" he repeated. "Now I can breathe again, laugh again, live again. Oh, God, thank You, thank You!" he whispered gratefully. With Cveja safe, all was well with his world.

"If anything calls for a celebration, this does!" Elizabeth declared. She rooted through the pantry and pulled out a dish of homemade pastries. Suddenly it almost felt like home. Elizabeth prepared a hearty meal, and they feasted merrily.

Two weeks later, a second message arrived from Cveja, this time a letter postmarked from Salzburg. Hurriedly, Voja slit the envelope open. Out fell a 100 Austrian schilling note. The letter read: "My dear brother, I found a job with an architect here. Would you believe it? He has twins, a boy and girl. And he said he'd have a job for you when you get here."

At long last they were making progress. Hope stirred anew in Voja's heart—God was on His throne, and all would be well.

Cveja had already received political asylum from Austria, but Voja still waited for his from Italy. Finally, on October 14, five months after arriving in Rome, he received his asylum papers. Since the authorities had kept his Yugoslav passport when he applied for asylum, he now requested a new passport. They told him to return the next day.

The next day Voja picked up what turned out to be a travel document for aliens, without which he could not travel. With that in hand, he went directly to the Austrian Consulate. He requested an Austrian visitor's visa to see his brother in Salzburg, and they issued it on the spot.

Overjoyed, Voja hurried home to pack his belongings in a larger suitcase that he had bought in hopeful anticipation of this trip. He had purchased a couple of shirts and another pair of pants since arriving in Italy, and his belongings wouldn't fit into the small suitcase he had brought from Yugoslavia.

"But how can you remain in Austria? They can't give you asylum, too," Djordje said, perplexed.

"I'll worry about that later," Voja replied. "I know only one country can grant asylum, but I can't think about that now, Djordje. All I can think about is seeing Cveja."

That evening, Voja bid his friends goodbye, notified his landlord, and made his way to the train station. The electric train that had brought him to Rome would now carry him to Salzburg. After five long months of separation, he would finally see his brother. He boarded a late train, but sleep did not come that night.

★ When King Miloš Obrenovic (MEE-losh Oh-BREH-no-veech) decided to visit his brother in Šabac, he was cautioned not to criticize the townspeople. The town had become known locally as "Little Paris" since it possessed the first hospital, pharmacy, and even the first piano in Serbia. Not surprisingly, the townspeople were quite proud.

But when the royal coach rumbled into the center of town and the people of Šabac surrounded him, the king forgot the warning as he stepped out of his coach and began a speech. Nevertheless, all went well until he got back into his royal coach and the horses started away.

The coach had gone but a short distance when, one by one, all four wheels fell off, causing the townspeople to roar with laughter. The king got out and stood by while the royal coachman retrieved the wheels.

The mayor of the town marched the two culprits over to the king. "Your highness," he said. "These men confessed and they want to return the linchpins they took. They didn't mean harm, just a friendly reminder."

The king looked at the men standing before him now. Just a few years earlier Serbia had won partial independence from the Turks. Suddenly he laughed and waved his hand. "We're a democratic country now. We're free, aren't we?" he said. "Let them go!"

CHAPTER 4

LEFT BEHIND

Cveja's Story

After Voja left for his tour of Rome and his planned defection, Cveja filled the void left by his brother's absence with frantic activity. The day after Voja's departure he took vacation leave from his job, and, with Voja's plans in hand, left Belgrade for Pirot. He would work on the architectural drawings there with the structural engineer. The pastor in Skopje had, in the meantime, decided to extend the church building, so he had even more work to do. On Wednesday, May 22, the date scheduled for Voja's tour group to return, Cveja was not in Belgrade.

Late that night Cveja phoned Grujica from a pay phone at a local post office. Grujica's stepfather had obtained a home telephone through his connections in the Communist Party. When the phone rang, Grujica had just returned from the train station, so he answered. As soon as he heard Cveja's voice, he broke down and sobbed.

"What's wrong, Grujica," Cveja asked. He didn't know for sure if Grujica had gone to the station. "You sound terrible."

"I . . . I got to the station early tonight, Cveja," he finally managed. "Voja was not on the train!" His sobbing resumed, and Cveja waited patiently. "I ran to every car. I looked everywhere. He just wasn't there!" More sobs. "Finally, everyone left. And then I saw someone with a name tag who turned out to be the tour guide." He sniffled between sobs. "The man told me that Voja disappeared. He vanished! Just like that!"

"It's okay, Grujica. Everything's okay. Voja is all right." Cveja spoke reassuringly, hoping it was true, but not knowing for certain that it was. "Voja planned to defect."

"Defect? Voja defected? But . . . how? Why wouldn't he tell me? Didn't he trust me?" More sniffles. "I cried all the way home." He paused. "You obviously knew, Cveja. Why didn't you say something?"

"I couldn't, Grujica. I'm so sorry," Cveja apologized. "Voja wanted to tell you but he wasn't sure how things would go. He had to be so careful. You understand that, don't you? Are you OK?"

Gradually Grujica began to calm down. "Yeah, I guess," he replied, still sniffling. "But I still wish you'd told me."

When Cveja hung up the phone, reality started to sink in. Voja—his other self, his shadow—was gone. He knew it for sure now, and suddenly he felt that his whole world had disappeared. He was left behind and alone.

For three weeks Cveja worked on the church project in Pirot. After completing the final architectural drawings, he returned to Belgrade. Arriving home, he found two letters waiting for him.

"This letter is from Voja," Nata exclaimed, her face beaming. For the first time in days, Cveja felt his heart quicken with joy. Like a breath of fresh air, word from his twin invigorated his spirit. Nata handed him an envelope. It was addressed to her and showed a familiar Croatian name and a Cento-celle return address. Nata had already slit open the envelope, so he pulled out the letter and read it eagerly.

"Dear Nata," the letter began. "Everything went well. I linked up with friends from Zagreb and found a furnished room. In the meanwhile, I registered with the Italian authorities and am waiting to receive asylum. I miss you and hope everyone in the family is well. With all my love, Brother Voja." He had written generically, but now they knew for sure that he had defected and was OK.

The other letter addressed to Cveja displayed the return address of the Uprava Državne Bezbednosti (Department of Internal Security). His fingers fumbled as he opened it and read the contents. The notice inside summoned him to their headquarter office.

The next day he went to the yellow stucco building that housed the UDBA office. Inside, he climbed the marble staircase to the spacious office where his brother had been interviewed weeks before. As he entered, two men looked up from behind heavy mahogany desks, one a civilian, the other an army colonel in uniform. The colonel motioned him toward a chair.

"So your brother betrayed us. He defected to the West," the shaggy-browed colonel began abruptly. "We educated him. Now he's gone to work for the capitalists." His voice was harsh, and he leaned back in his chair, glaring. "Write to him. Tell him to come back. Tell him we won't prosecute him if he returns."

"But how can I write? I don't know where he is?" Cveja replied. He did not actually have his brother's address.

"Is that so?" the man shot back with a smirk. He flashed a glance at the other man who watched in silence, legs crossed, arms folded across his chest. "Well, if *you* don't know, we do. We intercepted this letter to you," the colonel continued. He held up an air mail envelope and waved it too fast for Cveja to see the writing.

Cveja felt the blood drain from his face and his legs go weak. Rumor had it that UDBA agents operated in free border countries, sometimes kidnaping Yugoslav refugees off the streets and hauling them back. If the UDBA actually knew Voja's whereabouts, he could be in danger. Cveja also knew that the government monitored incoming and outgoing mail. The letter to Nata had slipped through, but it was possible they had found a letter from Voja addressed to him. Somehow, though, his instincts told him the man was bluffing. At least, he hoped so.

"You know that you and your brother are scheduled for military service in September, don't you?" the colonel went on. "You are to report to Carlovac for engineer officer training."

"Yes, I'm aware of that," Cveja replied.

For a moment, the colonel drummed his fingers on the arms of his chair, his eyes fixed intently on Cveja, his mouth drooping in a pout. Finally he spoke. "From now on, anytime you leave town for more than 24 hours, you are to inform this office. We want to know where you are, with whom, and how to reach you at all times."

The civilian, who had silently observed the interplay, now uncrossed his legs and unfolded his arms. He leaned forward and clasped his hands, elbows planted on the arms of his chair. "I've seen these fellows before," he said. "A couple of years ago they lived in an apartment behind my office. Every morning they exercised outside in the yard. I could see them from my window. They're identical twins—obviously very close. I'd wager anything this one will leave, too." He sat back and folded his arms again.

Turning back to Cveja, the colonel's dark eyes flashed. "I would advise you not to try that. It would be very foolish, you know. If you're caught, you would get a minimum of five years in prison, perhaps more. You'd be tried as an army deserter, and that's a serious matter."

Cveja left the office thoroughly warned but also thoroughly determined. The UDBA agent's threats—and presumed bluff—had only reinforced his resolve. If the man had intended to intimidate him, his scheme had backfired. Still, doubts about the letter and his brother's safety nagged him.

The next week Cveja returned to his regular job at the Hydroelectric Institute and collected his vacation pay. At the same time, he began to investigate ways of escape. Before leaving again for Skopje to complete heating, ventilating, and plumbing drawings, he called the UDBA office as instructed and reported his trip and itinerary. That evening when he arrived at the pastor's home, a surprise awaited.

"The UDBA called this afternoon," the pastor informed him. "They wanted to know if I was expecting you, and how long you were staying."

Cveja was taken aback. He hadn't expected them to verify his itinerary. "They must mean business. They're apparently determined to keep track of my movements," he said thoughtfully.

During the next two weeks Cveja finished the plans and submitted them to the church leaders in Belgrade. For all practical purposes, his work on the church project was finished. Now he needed to save up money for his expenses and formulate his plans to escape.

One day Cveja ran into the daughter-in-law of a lady from church who had rented a room to the twins after the authorities seized Mica's apartment and evicted the family. The twins had lived in that room until moving back in with Nata and Mica upon Mica's release from prison.

"The grapevine has been buzzing," the young woman said. "I hear Voja defected in Rome."

"It's true," Cveja replied, nodding, feeling a little uneasy. She and her husband were Communists, though somewhat disillusioned with the party. In the purge of 1948, when Tito broke with Stalin and all Russophile Communists in Belgrade mysteriously disappeared, her husband had vanished with them. No one knew his whereabouts until a year later when he suddenly showed up at home, unannounced and unexpected. During his absence, his mother prayed for his safe return. She had asked God to make it on a Sabbath, and that's when he reappeared.

"You probably don't know this, Cveja, but when Voja first applied for the trip, the UDBA called me. They wanted to know my opinion—whether I thought Voja would come back. I told them most definitely. He'd never leave his brother." She paused and looked him in the eye. "Evidently I was wrong."

As Cveja walked away, the woman's words replayed in his mind. He wondered to what extent her opinion had weighted the authorities' decision in Voja's favor. Shaking his head, he marveled at the many incidents that play out behind the scenes, yet come together like scattered pieces of a divine jigsaw puzzle. Gratefully he praised God for His intervention.

Sava, the twins' close friend and colleague, came by to see Cveja some days later. A mathematical genius, he had studied with them at Belgrade University, helping them prepare for the demanding and very difficult math exams which the vast majority of students failed on their first attempt. The Communist regime maintained very high standards for education since tuition was free. If students could not meet the standards, they could transfer to another field, learn a trade, or go back to farming.

"I think this is for you," Sava said, smiling as he handed Cveja an envelope. "It's addressed to me and shows a strange name and Centocelle address. But I recognized the handwriting."

"It's from Voja!" Cveja exclaimed, his eyes lighting up. He slit open the envelope and gulped down the words: "My dear brother, I'm still waiting to receive asylum. Things move very slowly here. Otherwise, I'm OK. In the meantime I'm learning Italian. I hope your plans are progressing. I miss you terribly and pray for you every day. May God be with you." He signed the letter simply, "Your brother."

"The minute I saw it I knew it was for you," Sava said. "Voja was smart not to write directly to you."

That night Cveja wrote back to Voja. He addressed his letter to the Croatian friends at the Centocelle address and left the return address blank. Then he dropped the letter in the mail.

Around the middle of July, Cveja reported to the UDBA his plans to visit his aging paternal uncle in Glušci for a few days. Cveja hadn't seen him for three years, and he yearned to visit his extended family and see the old homestead again. Uncle Mihajlo (Mee-HY-ylo) had gone to his rest in May, and only Uncle Milorad (MEE-lo-rahd), the eldest of his father's three brothers, remained. Milosav, the youngest brother, had been killed in World War I on the last day of fighting. Uncle Milorad was now 74 years of age and only slightly stooped from his former six-foot-five-inch height—he still towered over everyone else. During World War I, in the Kingdom of Serbia, he had served in King Peter's special guard which accepted only the handsomest and tallest of men.

As soon as Cveja appeared, four generations of relatives swarmed about him. He spent the night with his cousins, and helped the family thresh wheat the next day. Their threshing machine, which had replaced a larger one burned during a 1941 battle with the Germans, still operated efficiently. Cveja climbed to the top of a heap of sheaves beside the thresher and pitched sheaves down one by one to two cousins standing atop the machine. After slashing the binding twine, they fed the wheat stalks by handfuls into the noisy thresher. On one side of the thresher, wheat kernels spewed into sacks, while chaff, husks, and straw were expelled separately from other places on the machine.

"Look at the American work!" one of his younger cousins teased laughingly, as he tied up a sack full of wheat and another cousin replaced it with an empty sack. Without Cveja's saying so, his family instinctively knew he had come to say goodbye and that this was likely his last visit.

"*Ah, moj Aljo, crne oci. Ti ne lutaj svake noci* [Oh, my darling, dark eyes. Don't wander every night]," Cveja responded by stretching his arms wide and bursting into a familiar folk song. His clear voice rang out above the grating racket of the thresher. And as the others joined in, their voices swelled in happy chorus, working side by side throughout the day just like old times.

Later that evening Cveja and Uncle Milorad sat across from each other at one of the long wooden tables set out under the apple trees in the quiet courtyard. Though there wasn't as much land anymore, workers were still hired during threshing time to help each family with the crops on their allotted land. According to custom, workers were fed two meals a day at these tables along with the family members. Now all had retired to their homes, and the threshing machine rested idly until the morrow.

"I'm planning to escape," Cveja confided to his uncle.

"I knew you would," Milorad said sadly. "You have to follow Voja. You young people have to do what's best for your future. I'm the last of my generation, and I've seen so many changes. God only knows what tomorrow will bring."

"Tell me again, Uncle Milorad, about our family, how they came here, and what it was like." Cveja had heard the stories many times, but he wanted to take them with him—those stories were his heritage, the cherished values for which many of his people had died. Tales about the glories of their kingdom before the coming of the Turks, the uprisings, and the wars that finally set them free were passed down from generation to generation as were their ancient ballads.

"Freedom never comes cheap," Uncle Milorad began.

Except for a chorus of crickets humming in the background and a soft breeze rustling the leaves of the trees, all remained still as they talked. The sweet fragrance of early red apples nearly ripe for picking hung lightly in the cool evening air. Cveja drank it all in as he listened.

"That's the way it's always been." Milorad was winding down now. "Our small country always fighting more powerful enemies. They say that when a man fights to save his very existence, he'll fight harder and endure longer than someone who only wants to win. It must be so, I believe. Our history proves it."

Tears streamed down Milorad's cheeks as he searched Cveja's face. "When World War II broke out, you and Voja were too young to go to war. I hope you never have to." He paused, sighing deeply. "I will miss you, Cveja. You and Voja have been like my own sons."

By now night had fallen and the full moon flooded the courtyard with an eerie light, the strange shadows mute witnesses to their conversation. Basking in the memories of the past, Cveja spent another memorable day with the extended family and then returned to Belgrade.

One afternoon he made one last trip to Kalemegdan Park, seeking out the bench on the top terrace where Voja had broken the news that he had been approved to travel to Rome. That bench, chilly then in the dead of winter, felt warm now in the hot summer sun. Deep in thought, he sat there for a while and then walked to the black iron railing where he and his brother had stood that winter afternoon pondering their future. Cooing pigeons strutted around him now, as then, taking effortlessly to the air and fluttering back to the ground.

Far below, the waters of the two rivers mixed and mingled as before, flowing ceaselessly, always converging, ripples forming and vanishing. The dank, damp river air rolled up the bank and hung heavy around him. Breathing deeply, he tasted the promise of freedom once more. It was the same, yet altogether different. A sudden pang in his heart reminded him that his brother had flown away like the pigeons. With every breath, he ached to take flight, too.

Pausing at the foot of the towering Messenger of Victory memorial, he looked up at the bronze falcon. Its wings were still poised and ready to take off, hinting even now of freedom. Slowly he made his way out of the park and rode the trolley bus home alone.

CHAPTER 5

ENCOUNTER WITH THE BORDER

Soon after Voja defected, all the twins' friends had heard the news. They all knew it wasn't a matter of if Cveja would escape, but when. Some even offered suggestions.

"I visit Slovenia every summer. My mother's family lives in Jesenice. It's right on the border. I'm sure they'd be willing to help you," Mikica (MEE-kee-tsa), a female friend in Belgrade told Cveja one day in June when she saw him.

"It isn't that difficult to escape," someone else assured him. "There's a train that goes from Jesenice to Austria through a tunnel in the mountain. I saw it. All you have to do is sneak into the tunnel at night. You're young; you can do that. When you get out at the other end, you'll be in Austria."

"I can help you escape," Branko (BRAHN-ko), another friend living in Belgrade, promised. "I grew up in Jesenice. I know my way around. My wife and I will be leaving in a couple of days to visit with friends there. I could meet you and show you how to get to the border."

The border! What did Cveja, or anyone else for that matter, actually know about the border? He and his brother loved the study of geography, so they knew that Yugoslavia shared geographical borders with seven countries, most of them behind the iron curtain. Cveja certainly didn't want to end up there. Only two countries, Italy and Austria, were located in the free West. But he had no experience and no clue what to expect once he got there. All he knew was that others had escaped before him, and one of his friends had reported that crossing the border would not be difficult.

Filled with enthusiastic confidence, Cveja began to make preparations. He purchased a pair of comfortable hiking boots, pants, and a small backpack in which to carry a few necessities. Gathering his savings together, his vacation pay, and the money earned on the church project, he distributed his Yugoslav dinars among the socks he wore, his backpack, and the pockets in his jacket and pants. For emergency use, he wedged between the thick treads of his soles a US$20 bill folded into a tiny square and lodged a small pebble securely over it to hold the money in place. Finally he sent a postcard to Mikica informing her of his arrival time, signing it merely "Your friend."

A week later, on July 21, with a few necessities and a sack lunch prepared by Nata stashed away in his backpack, he bid a tearful goodbye to his mother and to Nata, Mica, and Jovica, and left for the train station. There he boarded the luxurious overnight Orient Express train that traveled from Istanbul to Paris, making a stop in Belgrade and a border stop in Jesenice.

This time he did not inform the UDBA of his trip. He would be traveling west, in the direction of the border, which would immediately arouse suspicion. He hoped that by now the secret police had become complacent. If he was lucky, by the time they noticed his absence he'd be safe in Austria.

At 6:30 a.m. the next morning, the train pulled into the station at Jesenice. Cveja found his friend Mikica waiting for him on the platform. Looking around he noticed that the police were everywhere. They were guarding the entrances to the train, checking passenger's papers, and following the crowd to scrutinize every individual. Afraid of drawing unwanted attention to himself if he lingered, he and Mikica walked away. They had not gone far when suddenly a horrifying scene played out before their eyes. A terrified young couple was being dragged away in handcuffs by armed border police. The woman was crying, the man protesting. Cveja watched aghast as the police hauled them off.

This was the last thing Cveja had expected to see. Physically, mentally, and emotionally, he was unprepared for the shocking reality. Shaken by the incident and the challenges confronting him, he wondered how his friends' reports could have been so wrong. Had they been merely speculating aloud? Expressing their own wishful thinking? His life and future were on the line here—why had he so naively believed them? The optimism that had propelled him to this place began to evaporate, and a terrible dread seized him.

Emerging from the station with Mikica, Cveja found himself in an industrial steel town nestled in a narrow green valley surrounded by an ominous wall of mountains. He had come from the flat plains of Macva, and the view before him was stunning. To the south and west rose the majestic Julian Alps; to the north, the Karavanke Mountains formed a natural boundary between Austria and Yugoslavian Slovenia.

"Where's the tunnel to Austria?" he asked as he gazed around at the unfamiliar sights.

"You can't see it from here," Mikica told him.

Together they walked down a narrow street bordered by steep-roofed houses and balconies overflowing with flowers. The initial shock gradually wore off, and Cveja began thinking clearly again. "I have to find a way to escape, Mikica," he told her. "There's no other way for me to leave the country. My brother is waiting for me. But I didn't expect the border to be so. . . so well guarded."

"You've come all this way, Cveja. Why don't you look around and investigate before you give up," she encouraged. "You never know what you might find."

Another disappointment awaited him when he arrived at her family's house. "We haven't found any leads for you, Cveja. At least none we could recommend and trust," Mikica's relatives told him. "Anybody can promise to take you across the border, but some of the guides work with the secret police."

Here was yet another danger he had not fully recognized. Nevertheless, when the family invited him to stay for a while, he accepted. He had decided to check out the town on his own—somewhere, somehow, there must be a way out.

As he wandered through the city the next day, Cveja came upon a used book store. While browsing around inside, he found a military map of the border. Though old and outdated, it indicated topographical configurations and border pockets. Those, he was sure, had not changed. If he crossed the mountains on his own, he needed to be aware of these boundaries.

"Most people can't read that kind of map," the shop clerk told him when Cveja inquired. "I have no idea where it came from." Cveja purchased the map and returned to the house.

He spent the rest of the day studying the map intently. He had heard reports of people he knew who had successfully crossed the border, but wandered into a pocket and back into the country where Yugoslav border guards arrested them and carried them off to jail. He couldn't let that happen to him.

Examining the map, he traced the border with his finger. It was just a meandering line of ink on paper, but in reality that line separated the captive from the free. Images of the young couple at the train station flashed into his mind. If the police caught him trying to escape, they would deal with him even more severely. Closing his eyes, he straightened his shoulders, drew a deep breath, and determined to press forward with God's help.

Late the next afternoon, Cveja met with Branko, his friend from Belgrade who had arrived in Jesenice two days earlier and promised to help him cross the border. Together they boarded a bus bound for the wide, grassy plateau at the base of the mountains overlooking the city. After the hour-long journey on the narrow roads winding through the rolling countryside, border police at the bus station greeted him and examined his ID.

Beyond the plateau rose the majestic Karavanke Mountains. Dense evergreen forests ascended the slopes and then disappeared into gray limestone crags at the snowy, rounded peaks. And somewhere on the other side of that mass of rock and snow was freedom.

Cveja eyed the lofty mountains above his head, even more visible and intimidating from this vantage point on the plateau. Mountains such as these had sheltered World War II resistance fighters from all regions of Yugoslavia who waged a guerilla war against their Nazi occupiers. And now here he was, engaged in a struggle for his own freedom—yet these mountains did not appear friendly to his cause.

Every so often, buses picked up and dropped off a few tourists. Police milled about, watching the new arrivals. Cveja and Branko ambled leisurely across the expansive meadow, admiring the colorful wildflowers and marveling at the panoramic view and the well-tended countryside. Looking back toward Jesenice, the view of the jagged Julian Alps in the south took their breath away.

As they strolled about, mingling with the tourists, Cveja took out a pair of binoculars to get a closer view of the awesome mountains and to see if he could locate the tunnel. Suddenly a policeman tapped him on the shoulder and asked for his identification again. Cveja pulled out his picture ID and told the man that he was visiting friends in Jesenice for a few days. He held his breath while the policeman eyed him, examined his document, then returned it and walked away.

From this elevation, some 4,000 feet high, Cveja could see the tunnel that plunged through the mountain. Austria and freedom awaited on the other side of that inaccessible hole in the mountain. Surveying the range, he noted that the mountains declined in height toward the east.

Presumably enjoying the scenery, he and Branko eased cautiously away from the crowd toward the eastern edge, taking care that no one noticed. About fifty tourists meandered about, and the police stayed busy following their movements.

Now the sun was setting on the horizon, and darkness began to fall. The two men seemed to have eluded the police and were out of sight of the crowd. All of a sudden Cveja saw it—a camouflaged structure built into the mountain. That must be where the border guards took their breaks. He realized that he was probably walking parallel with the border.

"Look, Branko, do you see that?" Cveja asked his friend. He pointed to the structure above them about 1,000 yards away.

"See what?" Branko said, squinting and looking side to side and then at Cveja.

"Up there. The *karaula*," Cveja replied. "Don't you see it?"

Branko shook his head. "No. Where? My eyesight isn't very good in the dark." Cveja was stunned. His life was in the hands of a man who had promised to lead him to the border but who couldn't even see well.

At that moment, Cveja remembered a news story he had read months before in Belgrade. The story in *Politika* reported that two Belgrade University students had fallen off a cliff while trying to escape over these same mountains at night. Their broken bodies were found days later and brought back to Belgrade. The recollection of this story froze him in his tracks.

"I think we'd better go back," Cveja suggested, thoroughly disappointed and frightened for both himself and his friend. Night was falling fast, and his eyes burned with unshed tears. He and Branko retraced their steps back to the plateau where a handful of tourists stood admiring the city lights illuminating the valley below.

On the bus ride back to Jesenice, Cveja sat sober and silent beside his friend, mulling over his experience. What was he doing wandering about on a mountain in the dark? How could he be so reckless? His actions were those of a desperate man. His friends' reports had proved to be rumors or speculations, not solid facts. Mikica's family had no information to give him. Even Branko had let him down. He shuddered to think what might have happened to them on the mountains in the dark.

The border was so near and yet so far away. Up there on the mountain he could almost smell the scent of freedom wafting across from the other side, enticing him and luring him onward. Yet he had turned back. Freedom might await him on the other side, but a mighty wall of rock and a host of dangers stood in the middle.

So which reports could he believe? Whom could he trust with his life? How would he escape?

"Thank You, Lord, for protecting the two of us from harm, and from the eye and ire of the police had they caught us," Cveja breathed in a prayer of gratitude. "And please help me find a way to escape and find my brother."

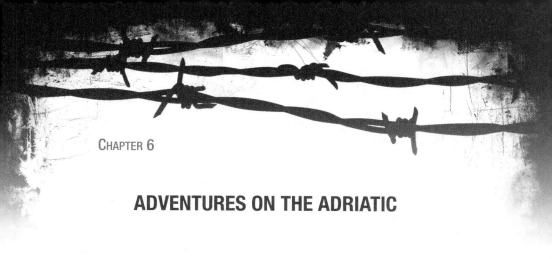

CHAPTER 6

ADVENTURES ON THE ADRIATIC

The next morning at Mikica's family's house, Cveja awoke feeling out of sorts. Sleep had not come to him until late and even then it was troubled. He had come here full of hope, but now he was shaken and filled with misgivings. Trapped behind these guarded borders, he knew it would be so easy just to give up.

As he prepared to leave Jesenice, he trusted the Lord to guide him, but had no clear idea where to go, who to turn to, or what to do. When someone mentioned that a mutual friend from Belgrade was visiting at Lake Bled, he decided to go there. It was only a short bus ride away. His friend traveled much and might have picked up some information along the way that could help him. Leaving some of his belongings at Mikica's family's house, he took his knapsack, said goodbye, and boarded the next bus to Bled.

Surrounded by forests and nestled in a mountain valley, the alpine resort was located a few miles southeast of Jesenice but still close to the Austrian border. Perched on the summit of a sheer white cliff, a medieval castle over-looked picturesque Lake Bled. A miniature island in the center of the clear blue lake was home to a church built in the 15th century. Cveja looked for his friend at the hotel address given him, but was told that the man had left that morning. After walking around the town and finding nothing promising, he checked into the hotel for the night. The next day he resumed his trip. This time he traveled south by bus toward the Italian border.

The bus route wound through several towns along the way. At each town he got off, scouted around, mingled with the locals, asked discreet questions, and listened for any possible encouraging clues. He stayed longer in some places than others, but in all he came up empty handed.

"Go to Nova Gorica [NOH-va GOH-ree-tsa]," someone in the last town suggested. "That's the best place to cross the border." Clinging to hope, Cveja boarded yet another bus.

In Nova Gorica a bizarre sight met him. An eight-foot wire mesh fence with barbed wire at the top sliced right through the middle of a street in the center of the city. The fence formed not only a border that divided the city in two but also an international border that divided two countries. On the Yugoslavian side of the fence was the newer city of Nova Gorica, built after World War II. On the other side lay the older settlement, renamed Gorizia when it was given to Italy after the war. Armed guards on both sides of the fence stood at huge gates spaced at regular intervals.

A line of people had formed at one of the gates. As Cveja watched, the gate slid open and a guard checked each person's identification before letting them pass through. Cveja felt a quiver of hope. If only he could slip in among the group. He watched until the guards closed the gate. It looked so easy.

It was dusk by the time he finally realized that he hadn't eaten all day. Lately, meals had taken a back seat in his priorities. He felt hungry now, and he sought out a café. Finding one, he went in and sat down. When the waiter came over, Cveja struck up a conversation with him. "Who are those people? How come they're allowed through the gates?" he asked, among other things.

"Only certain local residents have permission to cross," the waiter told him. "Some have relatives on the other side. Others go there to shop, or whatever. All of them are residents of this town."

Here in Nova Gorica he again encountered the border—more visible and seemingly more approachable than at Jesenice, yet just as impenetrable. The next day he inquired further.

"Every so often, someone tries to climb the fence and jump over to the other side," a resident told him. "They're shot before they make it." Sure enough, Cveja saw signs posted along the fence that served as a warning: "Danger," "Do not cross," and "Guards will shoot."

For two days Cveja walked around the town. He observed the gatekeepers and the people passing through. He noted when the gates were opened and closed. He tried to think of some way he might mingle in the group, some way to sneak through. With freedom so close, how could he not try? There must be a way, and he had to find it. But as he continued to deliberate and inquire, the feeling that had pervaded him in Jesenice returned. He was chasing the wind, ending up breathless but with nothing in hand. Disheartened, he left town. It was another failed possibility.

Now it was August. The last ten days of wandering had wasted precious time, energy, and funds. Cveja returned to his friends in Jesenice to pick up the rest of his belongings. He remembered hearing that his friend Željko had earlier escaped to Italy. Hoping to get some information from Željko's mother, he took the train to Zagreb on the second day of August.

"You can't stay here, Cveja," Željko's mother, Barica (BAH-ree-tsa), told him. "The secret police have been here twice already since Željko escaped. They may be watching the house even now. I'll take you to my sister Mica's [MEE-tsa's] house. You'll be safer there."

At Mica's house, Cveja rested for a while but he didn't want to just sit. He was consumed with an urgent need to plan his escape. Mica directed him to yet another house, this one belonging to the family of Željko's fiancée, Mira. When he arrived, Mira's mother, also named Barica, told him, "You can stay here, Cveja, but I don't have any information. The best thing would be for you to go back to Belgrade. We'll see what we can find out in the meantime. As soon as we learn something, we'll send you a postcard. We'll invite you to spend your vacation with us. That will be your signal that we found a connection."

Cveja returned to Belgrade. Overjoyed to see him alive and well, his family wrapped him in warm embraces. They had worried that he had been caught. All kinds of rumors were flying about, and they did not know what to believe. His mother and sister praised God for protecting him and for allowing them one more visit with Cveja.

"My soul, my pet, you're home now," Mother had simply said, smiling. She followed his every move with her eyes.

That night they discussed his predicament over dinner. "Haven't you been eating, Cveja?" Nata asked, noticing that his clothes hung loose on his frame. "Did you run out of money?"

"Sometimes I forget to eat. These days I'm not very hungry," Cveja replied.

"The UDBA hasn't called us," Nata reported. "Is it possible they didn't notice you were gone? Wouldn't that be something?"

"It would be a miracle!" Cveja exclaimed, relieved.

"How was it at the border? What did you see?" Mica plied Cveja with questions. He too was contemplating an escape.

"But where's my other uncle?" Jovica asked, happy to see one, but wondering what had happened to the other uncle who used to play with him.

Since the expenses of his trip had used up some of his funds, Cveja sold some of his clothing to a *komision*—an expensive pair of slightly used shoes, an overcoat in good condition, a couple of pairs of trousers, and three nice dress shirts. And then he waited for word from Zagreb.

Seven days later, the postcard from Mira's mother came in the mail. "Come spend your vacation with us," it said. "My daughter Branka will meet you across the street from the bus station. Be there at 10:00 p.m. on August 14."

Cveja was ecstatic. Finally, after all his disappointments and trials, something was going right.

"How do you intend to travel—by bus or train?" Mica asked when he heard the news.

"I haven't decided yet. The depots in Zagreb are near each other, so either will do," Cveja replied.

"I wouldn't take the train if I were you. Spies always travel the rails," Mica advised. "Buses are a little more expensive but less crowded. There's less chance of getting caught."

Cveja decided to take Mica's advice—he would go by bus.

As the day of his departure neared, Cveja called UDBA headquarters. He reported that he would be making another trip to Skopje on the church project. Skopje was south—Cveja would be traveling west.

CHAPTER 7

LICENSE PLATE H-8 . . .

Cveja arrived at the Belgrade bus station an hour early. After buying a ticket, he followed the signs written in Cyrillic and Latin scripts to the gate from which his bus would depart. The bus depot was not busy, and he was the first to arrive for the 4:00 p.m. Lasta bus to Zagreb.

The bus stood empty at the gate, doors closed, and he took his place at the head of what would soon become a line. Before long, passengers began gathering behind him. A bald, stocky, uniformed driver arrived, opened the door, climbed the steps, and settled into his seat. A second driver, a younger man, climbed the rungs of a narrow ladder on the side of the bus to the luggage rack on the roof. Passengers handed him their suitcases, and he secured them tightly with a strap. Cveja took his backpack with him and boarded the bus.

Selecting window seat No. 8, two rows back and directly behind the driver, he put his backpack on the shelf above his head and slid into the smooth black leather seat. A youngish couple boarded the bus, seated a little girl next to him in the aisle seat, and then slipped into the seats in front of him, directly behind the driver. The woman sat by the window, the man next to her. Cveja watched the rest of the passengers file onto the bus and shuffle past him to find seats. A middle-aged couple sat across the aisle from him.

After securing all the suitcases, the younger driver boarded, then leaned over and said a few words to the senior driver, who was writing something in a pad. The older man nodded. Then the younger driver took a seat on the front right side of the bus. The senior driver finished writing, put the pad in a compartment under the dashboard, adjusted the rear view mirror, surveying the passengers behind him as he did so, and checked his watch. Several minutes later, he checked his watch again. It was time. He turned the key in the ignition, looked to the left and to the rear, and pulled out of the depot into the street.

Cveja let out a satisfied sigh as the bus started down the road. Today, August 14, would be a date to remember. The tide that had run against him for so long was finally turning in his favor. Zagreb, 250 miles away, would be his stepping stone to freedom. A confirmed connection waited at the other end—a guide who would lead him safely across the border. No more running to and fro, searching, inquiring, and wandering around alone risking life and limb. That, and the prospect of an early reunion with his brother, charged every fiber of his being with hope. He checked his watch, and a wonderful sense of anticipation and relief flooded over him.

The bus wound through Belgrade's streets and soon left the city behind. Traffic on the two-lane *autoput* outside of town seemed lighter, and the bus sped toward its destination. Cveja sat back in his seat, breathing deeply, and watching the level landscape rush by.

The man in the front seat turned to check on his little girl, who was unbraiding her rag doll's brown wool hair. When Cveja looked at her and smiled, she clutched the doll to her chest and backed away. "What's your name?" Cveja asked, but she squirmed and kept silent.

"She's very shy," her father explained, then struck up a conversation with Cveja. "Going to Zagreb to visit?" he asked. "We're spending a few days there with my wife's relatives."

"I have friends there," Cveja told him. In the conversation that followed, the man told Cveja that he was an attorney. Cveja told him he worked at the hydroelectric plant in Belgrade and was taking time off from his job.

Passengers in the bus talked and laughed. A baby in the rear cried. The middle-aged man sitting across the aisle went to the back to visit with some of the other passengers. From his seat Cveja had a clear view of the road ahead through the front windshield. The bright sunshine outside reflected his sunny hopes and expectations. Yes, this was a good day. From all appearances, it would soon be even better.

Closing his eyes, he tried to unwind, to shake off the tension and stress of the past few months. But his muscles would not relax, and his mind would not rest. Recalling the message he had left with the UDBA only brought up images of angry agents hurling questions and demanding answers. "Why did you say you were going south? What were you doing heading west? Did you intend to betray us like your brother? What makes you think you could get away with that?" Since closing his eyes did not give way to rest, he sat staring straight ahead.

The bus stopped periodically during the trip, and the passengers got out for a short break. After one stop, the drivers exchanged places. Now the younger driver sat behind the wheel, and the senior driver moved to the seat on the right side of the bus. By now the sun had dropped low on the horizon. The driver switched on his headlights, and the bus continued its headlong rush into the night.

Before long, the lights inside the bus dimmed, the lively banter in the back quieted, and passengers began to doze off. The little girl beside Cveja turned sideways in her seat and fell asleep, legs drawn up, her doll entangled in her arms. Her mother glanced back at the girl, then repositioned herself in her seat with her head against the window. Cveja remained wide awake.

Some time later Cveja checked his watch again. The illuminated dial showed 9:00 p.m. Another half hour and he would arrive at his destination. He hadn't brought the postcard with him but he knew the address by heart. Hardly believing his good fortune, he kneaded his fingers together anxiously, yet excitedly. Things were flowing smoothly this time. Soon the bus reached the suburb town of Ježevo (YEH-zheh-vo). He could see the lights of Zagreb in the distance. Joy surged through his body.

Suddenly two bright lights on the road ahead caught his eye. An oncoming car, high beams ablaze, was speeding toward them in the other lane. As the car neared, its lights did not dim. Cveja sat bolt upright and stared at the onrushing vehicle. He watched aghast as the bus driver frantically blinked his lights to signal the driver of the car to lower his beams, but there was no response.

As the blinding lights raced closer, the desperate driver shielded his eyes and flashed his bright lights. In an instant, a blood-curdling sight appeared, and Cveja's heart stood still. A flat-bed Škoda truck piled high with sheets of steel was parked on the right shoulder of the road, the rear of the truck protruding into their lane. Blinded by the lights, the bus driver had not seen the truck until the last second.

Most of the bus passengers remained oblivious to the danger, but Cveja, wide awake, watched in stark terror. The driver swerved to the left to avoid plowing into the truck. But the oncoming car, lights still blazing, was almost in front of him now. The bus driver jerked the wheel sharply to the right to avoid a head-on collision with the car, but on the narrow two-lane highway there was no room to squeeze between the two vehicles.

Sleeping passengers, jolted awake by the bus's sudden erratic movements, screamed in horror at the sight that met their waking eyes. Suddenly there was a shrill screech and a whining roar, immediately followed by terrified screams, glass shattering, metal crunching, a deafening crash, and then deathly silence.

Just before impact Cveja had crouched down between the seats. Instantly he reached for the little girl but caught only her skirt. The force of the impact wrenched her little body from his grasp, leaving him with only a piece of her skirt in his hand. Everything had happened so quickly.

Sandwiched between the seats, he had been cushioned from the deadly blow and protected from a piece of steel that had passed only inches from his head. He pulled himself out from between the seats. The window on his left had been smashed, and the twisted frame hung grotesquely in the opening. Through the shattered windshield, he saw the oncoming car slow down.

Instantly he jumped out through the gaping hole on his right and ran around the front of the bus. Just three feet away, the driver of the oncoming car had stopped his vehicle. The man stared at Cveja as if he wanted to say something, but abruptly stepped on the gas and sped away, tires screeching loudly. Cveja screamed in outrage at the car as it swerved around the wreckage. "Idiot! Look what you did! Don't you see you killed us?" But it raced by without stopping, its bright lights still blazing into the night. He turned after it and watched it disappear. But he had recognized it as a Mercedes and noticed the first two digits of its license plate, H-8; the H standing for *Hrvatska* (Croatia).

Trembling, Cveja turned back to the bus and stared stupefied. The bus gaped open—the mangled mass of metal piled up, crushed together, and strewn across the road. It had slammed into the left rear of the unoccupied truck, and the impact had ripped away the right side of the bus and catapulted it at an angle across the road. Shattered glass covered everything in sight. He grabbed his head in horror and discovered glass shards in his hair. Glancing down, he noticed more glass clinging to his clothes. He could even feel it on his mouth when he licked his lips. He wiped the shards away with the back of his hand and spit.

By the beam of the one surviving headlight, he could see the Škoda truck, thrust off the road in the collision. Sheets of steel had pulled free from the load and were flared out in several directions.

When he looked for the alternate driver, he saw that the impact had flung him to the rear of the bus where he lay in a heap on one of the seats, staring ahead with unseeing eyes. The passengers on the right side had been thrown out of the bus by the impact and lay bloodied in the road. The mother in the seat directly in front of Cveja lay in the aisle, crumpled and bleeding, but alive and moaning. Her little daughter lay motionless in a small, bloody heap, her skirt shredded and her body broken and limp like the rag doll that peeked out from beneath her body. Farther back in the aisle, the little girl's father lay silent and still where he had been flung, a sheet of steel cutting into his body. The middle-aged man who had gone to the back of the bus to visit now wailed in grief at the loss of his spouse.

"Help me! Help me!" Desperate cries rose from the mangled mass of metal, rubber, and humanity. Surrounded by the stench of death, Cveja stood dazed and shocked, not knowing who to help first.

"It's not my fault! It's not my fault!" the young bus driver cried pitifully. Clutching his head in horror, he wandered aimlessly through the wreckage scattered on the road.

Cveja pulled himself together and set to work. He carried the still, small form of the little girl out of the bus and laid her in the grass beside the road. Then he rushed back in to carry out other passengers. Some stirred and got up, their clothing ripped by flying glass or cutting steel, their bodies and faces bruised and bloodied. Others rocked back and forth in an agony of fear and pain, wailing and crying aloud. Still others lay on the floor of the bus or sat slumped in their seats, unconscious or in shock. Splattered blood and shattered glass covered everything. The odor of spilled gasoline and burnt rubber tainted the fresh night air.

"Help me! Help me!" A cry came from beneath the twisted, mangled mess. Cveja and some of the minorly injured passengers began pulling at the wreckage to extricate the injured man. Behind him he heard a miserable groan. Turning, Cveja saw an elderly man trying to keep his eye in its socket. He and Cveja had conversed earlier. The man had come from Czechoslovakia to visit a friend in Zagreb. Nearby, a woman sat in her seat holding her jaw, her hands dripping with blood.

Scattered on the road and mingled with the debris were the trappings of human life. Suitcases were broken apart, their contents strewn about: a woman's coat, a baby's rattle, a handbag, a man's crushed hat, a crumpled paper lunch bag, a half-eaten apple, a lady's shoe with its heel broken off, a family portrait, a sealed envelope.

One by one, Cveja, the driver, and other passengers carried out the dead and injured. Some managed to sit up, others lay on the ground moaning, and some lay silent in death. Looking upon the carnage, Cveja felt dizzy and deathly sick. He never had been able to handle the sight of blood, and now it was everywhere.

By this time the highway blazed with flashing red lights. Three police cars had arrived on the scene, and the chaos was gradually brought to order. The police shut off the road, and traffic backed up in both directions. Ambulances from nearby hospitals screamed their arrival and began carrying away the injured. Cveja extricated his backpack from the debris in which it was lodged and slipped it over his shoulders.

"It's not my fault! It's not my fault!" the young driver continued to wail.

"I know, I know. The idiot wouldn't dim his lights!" Cveja responded, still angry.

"You saw what happened? Please, please tell them it wasn't my fault," he begged, pulling at Cveja's sleeve. "Be my witness. God only knows what they'll do to me."

Reporters and photographers swept in, and still the bus driver stuck close to Cveja's side. But how could he witness for this poor man? The UDBA expected him to be in Skopje. He was on the verge of escaping and could not allow himself to be caught. If the police found him on the outskirts of Zagreb, all would be lost. It would seal his destiny. He had to get away. But the bus driver would not let him out of his sight.

"This man saw it all. He knows it wasn't my fault," the driver told the reporters who questioned him. He pointed to Cveja. A female photographer pushed a camera in Cveja's face. He ducked when he saw it, and the flash went off with someone else in the picture. The worst thing that could happen would be for his face to appear in the papers.

A scene from Erich Maria Remarque's novel, *Arch of Triumph*, came to his mind. A Jewish doctor was hiding from the Nazis in occupied France.

When he knelt instinctively beside an injured person lying on a Paris street, he immediately realized his mistake. The next thing he knew, a German patrol officer tapped him on the shoulder and asked for his identification. When he could produce none, the officer led him away. That would be *his* fate, too, Cveja thought. The longer he lingered, the more perilous his situation became.

A reporter drew the driver's attention away for a moment, and instantly Cveja slipped away. Sliding down the incline into a ditch, he disappeared into a cornfield that stretched out alongside the road. The tall, tasseled stalks reached above his head.

In all the confusion, Cveja had lost track of time. When he looked again at his watch, the hands on the luminous dial showed 10:40 p.m., and he realized three things. First, he was alive. For that he was deeply grateful. Second, he was one of the few passengers uninjured in the accident. Had he been hurt, he'd be in an ambulance en route to the hospital where his identity would be discovered and his plan exposed. The Lord had mercifully spared him. Third, he had missed his appointment, and that awareness pierced his soul like a knife. At this point all he could think of was getting to Zagreb.

For a long time, Cveja sat on the ground in the cornfield, walled in by swaying leaves and fragrant tassels, waiting for the police cars and ambulances to leave and the traffic to disperse. He chastised himself for having taken the bus. Had he traveled by rail, he'd be safe in Zagreb now instead of hiding like a fugitive from the police. Finally he got up and plodded through the stalks, walking parallel to the highway but away from the accident. As he walked, his thoughts turned to the injured passengers. Before, when hearing of an accident, he had always counted the injured as fortunate for having survived, but now he had witnessed firsthand how serious the injuries can be. The images of mangled limbs, broken bones, and disfigured faces forever changed his perception of "the injured."

It was long past midnight when Cveja finally heard the voices of policemen clearing away traffic. "The highway is open. You may continue your trip." Motors quickly roared to life, and tires screeched as cars began rolling away. Still waiting in the cornfield, he could smell the exhaust fumes filling the air.

Cveja climbed back up the bank to the highway, emerging farther back where the cars had not yet begun to move forward. There in front of him was a Citroen, the license plate indicating a Paris registration since the last digits were 75. A man and woman sat inside the car, their attention focused on the cars in front of them.

Creeping up to the passenger side of the car, Cveja tapped on the window. The startled woman screamed at the sight of him—his clothes were torn and blood-stained, and shards of glass still littered his hair and clothes. In his best French, he told the couple that he had come from the accident and asked if they could take him to Zagreb.

"Certainment," the man promptly agreed, and Cveja got into the back seat. Traffic was moving slowly so it took them about an hour to reach the bus station downtown. Thanking the couple, Cveja got out of the car and they drove away. Inside the bus depot, he saw a number of late travelers, but no one waiting outside.

Standing there in his shirt sleeves, he shivered in the warm night air. His mind had gone blank, seemingly wiped clean of Mira's mother's address. Wandering about in a daze rubbing his brow, he tried to remember it. He knew the woman lived nearby, but for the life of him, he could not recall the name of the street, much less the house number. Frustrated and despairing, he spied a sign that read Kafana Dubrovnik, and he walked toward it. The café was closed and dark inside, but he sat down at an outside table, buried his head in his hands, and wept.

It was around 3:00 a.m. when his mind finally cleared and the address popped into his head. He was sitting only a few blocks away from the house he sought. Following the street signs, he soon found the house.

A knock at the door produced no sounds from within. Again he knocked, this time harder. "Who is it?" a small voice inside finally asked.

"It's me, Cveja," he replied.

"Cveja? Is it really you? One moment," the voice on the other side said. A few moments later he heard the lock turn, and Mira's mother appeared at the door. She took one look at Cveja and almost fainted. "What happened to you? You look awful!" she gasped, clapping her hands to her mouth. "Come in, come in."

Once inside, Cveja explained about the accident. He also told her that he had informed the UDBA he was going south. After she heard the story, she said, "Rest here for now, and in the morning we'll go to Željko's mother's house." She offered him food and drink but he only wanted water. After sleeping for a couple of hours, Cveja awoke at daybreak. The woman gave him a change of clothing that belonged to her husband, and they set out.

It was morning now, and the city streets were filled with people hurrying to work and with streetcars crammed with passengers. On a street corner, a young man peddled the morning news. "Extra! Extra! Get your morning paper! Read all about it! Bus collision on Autoput!" he shouted.

Handing the boy a few coins, Cveja purchased the *Vjesnik u Srijedu* paper. The front-page headline boldly reported: "Worst traffic accident ever on Belgrade–Zagreb Autoput." Wide-eyed, he scanned the details of the bus accident that had cost him his chance at freedom. The accompanying picture showed an unidentified man and the wreckage of the bus in the background. Cveja tucked the paper under his arm, and he and Mira's mother continued on their way.

While Cveja waited in Željko's mother's house, her sister Mica came over. Together the three women tried to locate a woman who supposedly lived on Trg Republica Street and was rumored to work as a guide, but they could not find her. He stayed overnight and picked up another paper the next day. "Witness Disappears. Wanted to Testify About Bus Accident," the headline announced. His stomach turned. The local police were looking for him, this time as a witness to the accident. Obviously it was not safe for him to remain in Zagreb.

CHAPTER 8

INTRIGUE ON THE COAST

Cveja gave his friends some money to buy him a new shirt and slacks since his own clothes were unwearable. Still shaken by the bus accident and his failed attempt to connect with a guide, he decided to go to the Adriatic coast to see if he could escape from there to Italy by boat. He took the bus from Zagreb to Rijeka (REE-yeh-ka), the principal seaport in Yugoslavia. The city sat at the head of Kvarner Bay on the Adriatic Sea, and in all the commerce and traffic there, he hoped to find some avenue of escape.

Screaming sea gulls wheeled overhead and waves lapped at the sea wall as he wandered along the waterfront, breathing in the odor of fish and salt water and watching freighters and passenger ships load and unload their contents. Out in the bay, he saw a cluster of islands in the clear blue-green waters. Somewhere out there was the island of Brioni, where Tito maintained a secret summer retreat. Out of view on the other side of the Istrian peninsula lay Trieste and Italy—and freedom.

Three days of traversing the city, listening, observing, and inquiring produced only a sun-burned face, aching feet, and more disappointment. Despite all his efforts, he had come up with nothing. However, many people living on the coast owned boats which they used to fish for food and earn income. Surely somewhere along this coast there must be someone who could help him escape. If he searched hard enough, long enough, he was bound to find that person.

A bus line ran along the coast, and Cveja decided to check out the towns along its route. From Rijeka he went to Pula, near the southernmost tip of the Istrian peninsula.

With its ancient Roman amphitheater, beautiful beaches, and pine woods, Pula jutted south into the Adriatic. When Cveja looked across the sea toward Italy, he could not see Italy's eastern coast because of the distance.

Perhaps because of that, he thought, the border might be less regulated by police. But after spending the day scouting the town, he came up empty. The next day he continued up the peninsula's western coast to Portorož.

Walking through the sunny seaside resort known as the port of roses, he did as before. He kept his eyes and ears open, checked out the place, struck up conversations with locals, and asked discreet questions. Here as elsewhere, his inquiries led nowhere. Not even one clue, one glimmer of hope, one lead that he could follow. It seemed he was beating the air and hitting nothing. Hope began to wither, and in its place he felt a growing sense of frustration and hopelessness.

Intent on leaving, he walked toward the bus station. An attractive young couple strolling in his direction suddenly stopped in front of him. "Excuse me, but aren't you Cveja?" the smiling young lady asked. "Don't you remember me? Last year I worked in Belgrade and sang in the church youth choir you directed."

"Elana! Of course. What a coincidence to meet you here!" Cveja said, surprised and elated to find someone he knew in this foreign place. Throughout his trip he had encountered only strangers. Now here was a friend.

"This is Romeo, my fiancé," she said, introducing her companion. "His parents live just outside of town. It's within walking distance. . . . Why don't you come along with us? We are on our way there. It will give us a chance to visit."

At the house the family greeted Cveja warmly and extended an invitation for him to stay for dinner. As they ate, they talked. "Romeo is Italian. He was able to get traveling documents for me," Elana told Cveja. "We'll be going back to Italy in a few days and getting married." Cveja congratulated the couple and, during the course of the evening, related his plight.

"It isn't easy to escape, Cveja," Elana said. She paused to think. "Now I did hear of someone. His name is, uh . . . yes, Giovanni Bartoni. Of course I can't vouch for him. All I know is that he has allegedly transferred people to Italy in his boat."

"Where can I find this Bartoni?" Cveja asked eagerly. His face brightened, and his spirit suddenly kindled with hope. After traveling around the peninsula, this was his first concrete lead. At this point, he was willing to try anything.

"There's a small café in Rijeka on the marina where the fishing boats moor. A lot of fishermen frequent the place. You might start your search there."

"But how will I recognize him? What does he look like?"

"Well, he's rather slim. Somewhat shorter than you. Maybe 40-50 years old. He's got a long face, and he's going bald. That's as much as I can tell you. I sure wish you luck."

"Since you've traveled so far, why don't you spend the night here?" Romeo's mother offered. "Tomorrow you can go back to Rijeka." Grateful, Cveja thanked her and accepted the invitation.

The next morning he prepared to leave. "If you need a place to stay the next few days, you're welcome to sleep here," Romeo's parents offered. "We'll be leaving tomorrow with the young people. The house will be vacant." She showed him where they kept an extra key. Cveja thanked them and left.

Back in Rijeka, Cveja went directly to the local church, which had a phone. The secretary in the office looked up the number for the café and placed the call for him. Cveja took the receiver. "Hello. I'd like to speak to Mr. Bartoni. Is he there?" he asked.

"One moment," came the reply.

A short while later, he heard a husky voice, "Bartoni here."

"I need to talk to you, Mr. Bartoni."

There was a long pause, then, "I was just leaving, but I'll be back later. Probably around 3 o'clock."

"Good. I'll look for you then," Cveja said and hung up.

When Cveja entered the café at the designated time, he saw six people sitting at three tables scattered about the small room. Three at one table, two at another, and one alone in the corner. Scanning their faces, he found only one fitting Elana's description of Bartoni—the man at the corner table drinking coffee and reading a newspaper. Cveja approached him. "Giovanni Bartoni?" he asked timidly.

Lifting his head, the man raised his narrow eyes from the paper and stared at Cveja. "And what if I am?" His bass voice had a deep twang. He laid his paper down and picked up his cup.

Cveja introduced himself and sat down. The tables closest to them were unoccupied, but still he proceeded in a cautious whisper. "I'm the person who called you this morning. I need to go to Italy."

The man raised his cup to his mouth and took a sip, his eyes still focused on Cveja. "And you think I can help you?" He licked his lips, slowly set the cup down, and leaned back. "Who told you so?"

"A friend." Cveja paused. "Well, can you?" Cveja thought the man looked and sounded like Humphrey Bogart. He had seen the actor once in the American film *Casablanca* when the university's student association obtained tickets. Due to the popularity of American films, tickets were hard to come by and getting one was a rare treat. Cveja felt as if he was in *Casablanca* now, deeply involved in intrigue. It felt strange and frightening, and he didn't like being in this situation.

"Do you mind?" Without waiting for an answer, the man reached for a pack of cigarettes in his shirt pocket.

Cveja shook his head although cigarette smoke made him sick.

The stranger lit up and inhaled, then slowly blew smoke out the side of his mouth and tossed back his head. "Forty-five thousand dinars," he whispered, leaning forward. Then he sat back in his seat, holding his cigarette to the side, watching Cveja's response. "Half in advance. The rest when we leave."

Cveja gulped. The amount equaled six months' salary. The average monthly salary at that time was somewhere between 6,000 and 10,000 dinars. "Can you tell me how you'll sail?" Cveja asked after recovering from the shock.

"Out of Portorož. I keep my boat here in Rijeka, but I sail between both places. We'll set out fishing after dark. There will be other fishing boats. I'll cast my nets; let the boat drift out as far as I dare. When I think it's safe, we'll row like madmen to the border markers—those red buoys out in the bay. We'll go under the cable. On the other side we'll be in Italian waters."

"Row? You're going to row?" Cveja frowned. He felt very troubled. "Your boat doesn't have a motor?

"I have no use for a motor." The man replied carelessly. He folded up his newspaper and placed his hands over it.

"Can you install one for this trip? You can sell it afterward and get your money back. I'd feel a lot better if you had a motor." Cveja waited breathlessly.

The man raised his eyebrows, took another sip of coffee, then put down the cup and exhaled loudly. "That will take time, my friend. And more money!" Leaning forward again, he paused, and then stated his price, "Another 45,000 dinars."

"Oh!" Cveja felt faint. "That's double the price," he mumbled. But he was desperate and at the end of his wits. "How long will it take?"

Bartoni thought a moment, eyeing Cveja. "Ten days. Be back here in ten days."

"All right, then," Cveja reached for his pocket to pay the deposit.

The man's hand shot out and grabbed Cveja's arm. "Not here. Meet me in Portorož." Slowly he withdrew his hand. "I'll be in the men's bathhouse on the beach. Tomorrow at noon."

Cveja nodded and left, the arrangements made. Walking out the door, he heard Bartoni call out an order for another coffee.

The next morning Cveja took the bus to Portorož and arrived at the beach early. He wanted to be sure he could find the bathhouse in time. In the morning sunlight the sea shimmered azure blue and several people frolicked in the surf. When he entered the men's bathhouse, Bartoni was leaning against the wall, legs crossed, puffing away on a cigarette. When Cveja entered, he turned and raised an eyebrow, then blew smoke out of his mouth.

"It's OK. No one's here," he said, noticing Cveja nervously looking around. His voice sounded calm. Snuffing out his cigarette in the sink and depositing the stub in the waste can, he moved to the entrance, looked around outside, then shut the door. "All clear."

Cveja handed him the 45,000 dinars, half the money he owed. Bartoni counted it quickly and pocketed the wad. "Do I get a receipt?" Cveja asked.

"A receipt?" The man laughed. "That would incriminate both of us if the police found it."

"Oh! I didn't think about that," Cveja said, somewhat embarrassed.

"You'll just have to trust me." Bartoni narrowed his eyes.

"OK, I understand," Cveja said, after a pause. "So I'll see you again in ten days?"

"Ten days it is," Bartoni confirmed. Resuming his former position, he pulled another cigarette out of his pocket. He nodded toward the door. "I'll leave after you do. It's not a good idea for us to be seen together."

The agreement entered into, Cveja left. Though he felt a twinge of panic, he was willing to take the chance. This was, after all, his only option. Walking away from the bathhouse, he felt a rush of excitement as he inhaled the fresh salty air.

A promenade bordered by fragrant flowers wove along the lovely coast, and he decided to take a stroll. As he sauntered along the concrete path, his mind danced with thoughts of freedom and his brother.

With a satisfied feeling of accomplishment, Cveja started toward Romeo's family's house, intending to spend the night there. But his thoughts kept returning to Bartoni and how he would sail. Curiosity about the distance to Italy egged him on. Portorož was about as close to Trieste as he could get from this side of the border, but Piran perched farther out into the Adriatic on the northwest tip of the triangular-shaped peninsula. He wondered if he could actually see Trieste from there. It would be such a wondrous sight. Since Piran was just a short distance away, he decided to investigate and boarded the next bus.

Picturesque Piran, some of its medieval walls still preserved, was backed by hills and mountains like most of the towns along the Adriatic coast. By the time he arrived night had fallen, and he found the beach nearly deserted. A few residents wandered along the beach walk.

As Cveja strolled along the narrow beach, he noticed intermittent brilliant flashes of light that swept across the beach and lit up the bay. Watching carefully to trace their source, it seemed to him that the beams originated from a building on top of the hill. Tomorrow during daylight he would solve the mystery.

After spending the night in a local hotel, he rose early the next morning and climbed the hill. It was not steep, and he soon reached the top. On its crest stood an old Catholic church with a square Venetian-style bell tower. *This is the source of the light,* Cveja thought. *The beams came from the top of this tower.*

The entrance door was unlocked, and he walked into the church narthex. On the right, he found a door which he assumed led to the tower. Opening it, he entered the narrow enclosure. Inside, darkness engulfed him. He felt his way up the steep, narrow staircase to another flight of stairs and another door. It, too, was unlocked. Beyond the door, another steep staircase rose upward, ending at the ceiling. He climbed to the top and found a hinged access door. *Just like the door to the attic pantry in our farmhome,* he recalled.

Cveja pushed hard at the door. It lifted up and daylight flooded over him. When he peered out, he was looking straight at a pair of army boots.

His gaze traveled up the legs of the uniformed guard to the stunned look on his face and then to the rifle he was pointing directly at Cveja.

"Come out, come out. What are you doing here?" the guard demanded. "Are you a spy?"

"A spy? No! Of course not!" Cveja replied, at once both shocked and terrified. He stumbled out and let the door drop behind him with a bang. "I'm a tourist. I saw the tower and wanted to see the view from up here." Through the arched openings of the belfry Cveja could see a white line of surf on the pebbly beach and a spectacular view of the bay. But it was the view inside the tower that left him reeling. A giant rotating reflector sat on the floor. At two of the four arches, machine guns set on tripods pointed out toward the beach.

"This is a military zone. A restricted area. Didn't you see the sign outside?" the guard continued, still clutching his rifle.

"A sign? No, I didn't," Cveja said, his mind racing as he tried to comprehend the situation. "Last night I was on the beach and noticed lights coming from this direction."

"How did you know they came from here? Let me see your identification."

"I simply observed. It wasn't hard," Cveja explained, reaching into his shirt pocket and pulling out his identification card. He handed it to the guard.

The man leaned his rifle against a box, examined the document, and then gave it back. "I see you're from Belgrade," he said. He took up his rifle again.

"That's right. I've been to the coast only once before. It's so beautiful," Cveja replied, trying to make conversation. "And where are you from? You don't sound like a local."

The guard relaxed. "I'm not. I came from Belgrade, too," he said. "That's my home. I've been stationed in this location for a year now. I monitor the border."

Cveja gulped hard. He had inadvertently stumbled into a government security post that guarded the sea border. From here, he had an inside view. When Bartoni took him out in his boat at Portorož, he'd be on the outside, maybe even on the receiving end of bullets from these very guns.

"Italians cross the sea boundary all the time," the guard continued. "Apparently there's more fish on the Yugoslav side. We have more islands along our coast than they do. Sometimes I have to use the loudspeaker. Then the coast guard goes out and brings them in. They get fined, but still they return."

"I never thought that would be a problem," Cveja said. He noticed the binoculars hanging around the guard's neck.

"Of course, I also monitor the border going out. I can see the entire bay area, here in Piran and also adjacent Portorož. Most of the boats out there are fishing boats. They usually go out after dark. My instructions are to shoot anyone who gets too near the border markers in the middle of the bay."

Cveja shuddered, especially at the mention of Portorož. "Sounds like you've got everything under control," he said quickly, trying to quell his panic. "Thanks for letting me see the view." He pulled up the door and stumbled down the stairs. There at the side of the road was the sign, "No Trespassing. Military Area." *How could I have missed it,* he wondered.

As he descended the hill, he muttered to himself. *Downhill. My efforts are going downhill again. Just when I think I've got a solution, something goes wrong. How could Bartoni promise to take me across? He must know the sea outlet is guarded. Escape is very risky. It seems impossible.* Cveja's hope withered away. He took the first bus back to Rijeka.

Bartoni was not at the café when Cveja arrived, so he sat at the corner table, ordered a glass of juice, and waited. Before long, the door opened and Bartoni entered. Cveja caught his eye. When the man joined him, Cveja related his experience in Piran.

"It looks very dangerous," Cveja said.

"It is!" Bartoni replied. He seemed unperturbed.

"They have reflectors that light up the entire bay. Machine guns, too," Cveja said.

"I know."

"Have you ever done this before? Taken someone across?"

"Yes, but not recently."

"They can shoot at us. We could be killed."

"They can't shoot on the other side of the markers. Two people in a boat, fishing, won't raise their suspicions. They won't notice what we're up to until it's too late." He tried to calm Cveja's fears.

Cveja left, wanting to believe Bartoni but only half convinced. It appeared too risky, too dangerous. But what were his options? He had no other choice. He would have to trust this stranger and hope and pray for the best.

After meeting Bartoni he checked into a small hotel. Feeling tense and edgy, he decided to take a walk before turning in for the night. A walk would work out some of his tension and restlessness.

Not far from the hotel he ran into a church member he had met previously in Rijeka and in whom he had confided his predicament. Seeing Cveja now, the man cautioned him. "I don't think it's a good idea for you to sleep in the hotel. But don't cancel your room either," he said. "If the police are on your trail, they'll focus on catching you there. Come with me, I have a shed in my vineyard. It's clean and has a bed. You can sleep safely there," he offered. Cveja accepted and walked with the man back to his place.

Seven days remained before Cveja's departure, and his money was running out. When he counted it, he had 20,000 dinars left, nowhere near enough. He still owed Bartoni another 45,000 dinars. He would have to borrow money. He thought of his friend Ladi (LAH-dee) who lived in Novi Sad and decided to take the bus there. That night he slept again in the church member's shed, and the next day he left.

Since the bus to Novi Sad made a stop in Zagreb, Cveja decided to drop by to see Željko's mother. She had been so kind to him on his previous visit when she, her sister, and Mira's mother had embraced him as a son and tried to help. When he arrived, she met him with shocking news.

"It was in the papers, Cveja, just after you left!" she said excitedly. "The report said there were three people in the group, a man and two women. They met up with a lady guide at the train station and she took them to Maribor in Slovenia. Another guide was supposed to meet them there. But when the four of them got off the train, who should be waiting but the secret police?" She wrung her hands and sighed. "Can you believe it, Cveja? The police tried to arrest them, but the man pulled a gun and shot one of the police agents. The second police agent shot him back, and both men died. Then the agent arrested the two women and the lady guide. When they went to the guide's apartment, they found a stash of dinars and U.S. dollars. But that isn't all. That night the lady guide hung herself in prison with her nylon stockings."

Cveja listened in shocked silence, too thunderstruck to respond. It was the group he had come to Zagreb to join, but the bus accident had prevented him from meeting them.

"Just think, Cveja," she was saying. "If you hadn't been in the bus accident, you would have been there with them. You'd be in prison today—maybe even dead."

Cveja stared at her. Weak and unable to speak, he was humbled by the revelation. The tragedy that had seemed so disastrous to his plans at the time had actually spared him from an even worse fate. "Oh, Lord, You saved me again. Thank You, God. How strange are Your ways," he prayed silently. "Help me to always trust you no matter what." He spent the night at her house and in the morning resumed his trip to Novi Sad.

When Cveja arrived at Ladi's house, a warm welcome awaited him. Luckily for Cveja, Ladi had remained home, although it was Sunday and the church members were having a picnic. Cveja told him about the startling events of the past several days.

"Man, you're making your guardian angel work overtime!" Ladi said. "But something tells me you didn't come all this way just to tell me your story."

Cveja smiled. "Am I that transparent? You're right, Ladi. My money will soon be gone. I know it's a lot to ask of you, but I need 45,000 dinars. You know I'm good for it."

"Of course, my friend," Ladi replied. "Let me see what I can do." He went into another room and returned with a handful of paper dinars. He counted them out. "Here's 50,000. Return it when you can." He pressed the money into Cveja's hand, refusing to accept an IOU. "The extra 5,000 is so you'll eat. You look like you haven't been doing much of that lately."

"You're a lifesaver, old friend. I'm forever in your debt," Cveja replied, hugging his friend. "And you know I'll return it as soon as I can." Ladi invited him to stay a couple of days. Since the boat was not ready yet, Cveja accepted the invitation.

The next day Cveja looked up some close friends who lived in Novi Sad. When he arrived at their house, Kaca (KAH-cha) answered the door. They had known each other for years because the Novi Sad and Belgrade church youth choirs often performed at each other's churches. While they visited she told him that her fiancé, Djoka (JOH-ka, a version of Djordje), and his younger brother had managed to obtain passports in order to attend a work-related trade exhibition in Paris. While there, they defected. When their father left for Paris to get treatment for a war injury, and to bring them back, he didn't return either. The UDBA were furious. Now she, her future mother-in-law and another brother of Djoka's remained behind with no hope of ever leaving the country legally. Kaca was desperate.

"When you escape, Cveja, please promise you won't forget us," she begged. "Please send us the name of your connection. You can write to Djoka in Paris." She wrote down the Paris address on a piece of paper and handed it to Cveja. "He'll inform us in the usual way."

"Of course, Kaca," Cveja promised, pocketing the note. "As soon as I get out, I'll write to Djoka."

The next day Cveja returned to Rijeka, taking with him the borrowed money. That night he slept in the shed in the church member's vineyard. After dark the following day he walked to the marina. He wanted to see Bartoni's boat since only two days remained until his appointment.

The skiff bounced in the ripples at its mooring, space No. 6. Bartoni had given him the number. A tarp covered it completely, and Cveja lifted it up to peer underneath. It was a beautiful boat, and inside he saw ropes, a box presumably containing baits, a water jug, cast nets, fishing poles, and other fishing gear. Most important of all, he saw a shiny, newly-installed motor. Elated that Bartoni had followed through, Cveja's optimism surged, and he pushed away his doubts. So far, the man was on target. Perhaps his fears were unfounded and Bartoni was right.

When Cveja returned to the shed in the vineyard he found the owner waiting anxiously for him.

"Oh, Cveja, Cveja, I've got terrible news!" He grabbed Cveja by the arm. "At the end of prayer meeting tonight the church secretary cornered me. She looked very upset. She said she has a friend who works as a clerk in the local UDBA office. She's not a Communist. The secretary had mentioned Bartoni to her once. On the friend's own initiative, she looked up Bartoni's file." The man paused to take a quick breath. "There's more. When she looked in the file, she saw *your* name. *Your* name was in Bartoni's file!" he repeated.

Horrified, Cveja stared at the man, all hope dying inside him. He remembered talking with the secretary when he had asked her to place the call to the café. Evidently she had taken an interest in his situation and talked with her friend.

The man continued, "Her friend said that Bartoni was in prison twice for smuggling people out. Now he collaborates with the police as a way of rehabilitating himself. She said he would take you out in his boat and act surprised when the coast guard surrounded you. Afterward they'd all divide your money between them. She said it was urgent that I let you know."

"Oh, no!" Cveja exclaimed, shocked and perplexed by the news. "How can she say that? Is she sure? He already installed the motor."

"She wouldn't say something like that if she weren't positive. He's a con man, Cveja. That's how he works. You can't trust him."

Cveja felt faint. He covered his eyes with his hand. "I already paid him half the money."

"Forget the money," the man urged. "You have to leave Rijeka immediately. The UDBA are planning to arrest you."

Despair overwhelmed Cveja once again and sucked the very life from his soul. Again his plans had been thwarted, his hopes crushed. "It's late now. Sleep in my shed tonight and get some rest," the man suggested. "You'll be OK here. Tomorrow you can leave."

Early the next morning Cveja made his way to the bus station. It was busy at that time of the morning, and in the crowd that milled about the depot he spied the familiar face of a friend, a medical doctor from Zagreb. He was walking toward one of the gates as Cveja hurried to catch up with him.

Putting his hand on the man's shoulder, Cveja exclaimed, "Vlado, my friend, where are you going?"

Vlado turned around and smiled. "Cveja, old man! What a surprise to see you," he said. "I'm on vacation, going to Split. And you, brother? What are you doing in these parts?"

"I'm in big trouble, Vlado." Cveja pulled him aside and briefly related his dilemma.

"Do you know who escaped a few days ago?" Vlado queried. "Mira, Željko's fiancé. She went to Austria."

"I hadn't heard," Cveja replied. "I'm desperate, Vlado. I've exhausted every lead, and I need a connection. Is there any way you could help me?"

"Hmmm, I really can't think of anything—unless Mira's mother has information." He paused. "I have a brother in Pula. He's a shipyard engineer. He works as a chief engineer for the production of ship motors. He might have some ideas, or perhaps he could put you in touch with someone. Here, I'll give you his address."

Vlado put his suitcase down and pulled a prescription pad from his inside coat pocket. Hastily he scribbled an address. "I'll give you a letter of introduction." He continued writing. "Give this to my brother." He tore off the sheet and handed it to Cveja, then put the pad back in his pocket, picked up his suitcase, and hurried toward his bus. While they had been talking, a line of passengers had formed at the gate and were now boarding the bus.

"Thanks so much." After waving as Vlado rushed away, Cveja quickly read the note. "Dear Ivan, This is my dear friend and colleague. He wants to leave the country. If there is any way you could help him, I'd be grateful." It was signed Vlado. Instead of proceeding to Zagreb, Cveja took the bus to Pula.

The address on the paper led Cveja to an attractive row house with several steps up to the front door. In front of the house sat a shiny new Vespa Moped, rarely seen in Yugoslavia at that time since most people could not afford one. Cveja walked up the steps and rang the bell.

The door opened and a dignified-looking man stood in the doorway. "I'm Cveja Vitorovic , a friend of your brother Vlado," Cveja told him.

"My brother? Yes, do come in," Ivan said, his manner cordial. "I just returned from six months of advanced training in France." He chuckled. "As you can see, I bought a moped there."

"Now what can I do for you?" he asked when they were seated.

Cveja handed him the note, and the man read it silently.

Lifting his eyes from the note, he dropped his hand to his side and replied. "I'm sorry, my friend, but I can't help you. From time to time I sail to Trieste and back on short trial runs to test a new diesel motor. I could try to get you in as a trusted guest, but unfortunately, we have no runs scheduled for the near future. None at all."

Cveja's heart sank. He had so hoped for a breakthrough. Another door slammed shut in his face. "Thank you, Ivan, for your trouble," he said, hiding his disappointment. "Sorry to have bothered you." They shook hands, and he left. He walked straight to the bus station and departed on the next bus to Zagreb.

CHAPTER 9

ESCAPE IN THE NIGHT

Cveja arrived in Zagreb feeling like a wounded soldier fresh from combat at the front. Since his first attempt to escape in Jesenice, he had run from one place to another for almost two months, fleeing like a fugitive or a hunted animal and almost never sleeping in the same bed twice. What did he eat? Where did he sleep? How did he live? Where did he bathe? Who did he see? It was all a blur now. Everything he tried had failed. Every hope of success had crumbled, and uncertainty and danger pursued him like a plague. Life felt like a runaway train out of control, and he couldn't put on the brakes.

Voja had left for Rome in the middle of May. It was September 5th now, and the crisp fall air had already replaced the heat of summer. Success was no closer now than when he had started. Before long the trees would discard their leaves, making an escape across the border more dangerous without the protection of their cover. In less than three weeks, on September 24, he was scheduled to report to the military. If he didn't escape before entering the service, it would be too late to go to America when he got out. If Mira's mother couldn't help him now, he didn't know what he would do or where he would turn.

"I'm sorry, Cveja. You can't stay here," Mira's mother told him when he arrived. His heart dropped, and his last reserve of hope ebbed away. "The police have already been here twice since Mira left. They may still be watching the house. Let me take you to Željko's mother's place."

After nightfall, weary and disheartened, he accompanied the woman to Željko's mother's house. "You can stay in my house, Cveja," she offered. "My sister Mica may have a good connection for you. Her husband knows a man, a Slovene. But we won't be sure until tomorrow."

The next day Hans the Slovene appeared, visting from Hodoš (HOHdōsh) in Slovenia. "I'm going back on Monday," he told Cveja. "I'm not the guide but I'll turn you over to him there. He's Hans, like me, a relative of mine. If you have the money, you can come with me."

If you have the money, you can come with me. The man's words fell on Cveja's ears like a beautiful blessing, a promise of deliverance. The dark clouds of despair seemed to part, allowing the sun to shine through once more. Yes, he did have money, the money he would have paid Bartoni. Cveja gave Hans 2,000 dinars as a deposit, with the remaining 60,000 to be paid to the guide.

On Sabbath, September 7, while Cveja remained hidden in the woman's house, she went to church. "I saw Pastor Radoš Dedi from Belgrade today," she reported upon her return. "He came to preach, and we talked after church."

"So what did he say?" Cveja asked eagerly. "Did he know anything about me? Did he say anything about my family?"

"He said your sister Nata signed the registered-mail notice for the military for you. The UDBA called the church and talked to him. They consider you an army deserter now. He said they promised him that if you turned yourself in, they'd forgive all. They said copies of your picture are circulating at all the borders. He asked me if I had heard anything about you."

"Well, did you tell him?" Cveja asked.

I wanted to, Cveja, but I wasn't sure if I should," she said. "The less said, the better sometimes. So I decided to say nothing. Did I do the right thing?" she asked.

Cveja assured her that what she had done was fine. She was trying to protect him.

Early on Monday, Hans came by. That same day he, Cveja, and Marko, a young man from Montenegro, left by train for the northeastern corner of Slovenia. Cveja's previous efforts to escape had been concentrated in the northwestern part of that Yugoslav republic.

It was September 9 now, the twins' twenty-eighth birthday—their first spent apart. The hollow feeling in the pit of his stomach told him that a part of himself was missing. As he waited to be escorted across the border, he wondered what his brother was doing that moment in Rome. How was he surviving? Did his heart ache too? Did he have any idea what Cveja was going through? Would they ever see each other again? As the train rushed him to his destination, a tingling joy began to course through Cveja's veins in anticipation of success. Already he could envision his brother's smiling face.

When the three men arrived in Murska Sobota, Hans hailed a cab that took them to the restaurant where they were to meet their connection, the other Hans. It was 11:00 a.m., and the lunch crowd was beginning to gather. Cveja had no idea who to look for, but the man led them to a table to order lunch.

As they waited for their food, a tall, stocky man with straw-colored hair approached. The first Hans poked Cveja in the rib and then nodded to the man standing before them. Cveja stood up. Hans greeted and embraced him and Marko as if they were family. The first Hans left, and the three remaining men chatted over lunch. Anyone looking on would assume that Cveja and Marko were Hans' nephews. They remained there until dusk and then took a cab to Hans' house in Hodoš.

The house sat behind a plowed-over field sprinkled with haystacks. A small orchard spread out in the rear, the silhouette of trees visible in the dim light. Inside the house the three men sat around the kitchen table talking while Hans' wife prepared a meal of homemade cheese, dried meat, dark bread, and fresh plums and apples from the orchard.

"I have a small field about seven miles west of here. It's practically on the Austrian border," Hans explained. "The authorities allow me to work there during the day." His mouth turned up on one side in a sly smile. "Many times I've gone there at night to observe, to watch the border guards and jeep patrols."

Cveja and Marko listened intently since their lives depended on this one conversation.

"When we leave here, we'll follow the road that runs northwest toward the Austrian border. You need to be watchful and cautious. Silent, too. A border jeep randomly patrols the road." He paused to be sure they understood and then continued. "When we get to 'no man's land' near the border, the guards can shoot without giving a warning. We'll be crossing at the *tromedja* of Yugoslavia, Hungary, and Austria." The look on his face grew intense and he leaned forward, pushing back a stray lock of hair. "The guards always patrol in pairs. There's a narrow gravel path on top of the embankment. Every two hours they change shifts. They take a break and go into the *karaula* for a drink or smoke and to report to their replacements. During that brief interval the border is unguarded. That's when we move. We have ten minutes to cross. When I say, 'Now!' run like the devil and don't stop!" Biting his lip, he sat back and folded his arms.

As they conversed, he described other features of the border and their route and gave them additional instructions. Eventually the conversation turned to where they'd spend the night. "UDBA agents are everywhere," the man said. "I can't let you sleep in the house." He led the two men outside. Darkness had fallen, and the moon shone clear in the cloudless sky. "Later tonight I'll go to the field and verify the schedule once more. I want to be sure it hasn't changed before we set out."

He showed them to a small barn. "One of you can sleep here. There's plenty of hay in the loft." Marko took the barn. Hans led Cveja to a large conical-shaped haystack about ten feet high. "There's a dugout under this stack," he said. He squatted down to clear away some loose hay at the base, revealing an opening. Then he stood up and gestured for Cveja to climb in. "It's really not bad. Now try and get some sleep."

Cveja looked at the man uncertainly and then stooped to crawl into the hole under the huge stack. He found the cavity quite large, about three feet deep, and straw-lined. When he got in and stretched out his legs, his shoes touched the end. A wooden structure overhead inside the stack prevented the hay from collapsing on top of him.

Lying there stretched out like a statue, Cveja stared into the darkness. Scooping up slivers of straw, he let them fall through his fingers. The familiar odor of hay inside the stack transported his thoughts back to his childhood farm home. Only the scent was familiar though. The hay itself, like the straw of this strange bed, was foreign. How small his world had become—this haystack, this hole in the ground, this night. What was he doing here so far from home, so desperate and alone? Finally his tired body succumbed to exhaustion, and he slept.

The next day Cveja and Marko gathered in Hans' house for a report on his visit to the field. "The guards' schedule has not changed," he said. "At exactly 3:00 a.m. they change shifts. That leaves a 10-minute gap." Cveja and Marko spent the entire day secluded in the man's house. Although they were out in the country, they didn't want to risk drawing the attention of suspicious eyes.

After dark the three men went outside. "Tonight we will leave," Hans said. "I'll wake you up at midnight. Have a good rest."

That night Cveja lay anxiously in his underground cocoon, his body tense with anticipation. It was September 11 already. Everything depended on the events of this night. He sifted through the possible outcomes: by morning he would either be a free man in Austria, arrested at the border, or dead. Even now the cold, dank hole reeked of the soil and the grave. He was depending on the goodwill and judgment of a stranger who held his life in his hands. Others had failed him before. If the Lord was not with him now, all would be lost. The words of Tolstoy surfaced in his mind. "Man is only free when he is reconciled with death." Was he ready to die? *No!* he decided quickly, hoping it wasn't his time. Listening to the night sounds and his own regular breathing, he eventually drifted off to sleep.

It seemed that he had just fallen asleep when the sudden sound of footsteps hurrying toward him startled him awake. "It's time to go!" a voice outside called softly. Cveja sat up and crawled out of the hole, slivers of straw still clinging to his jacket and pants. His heart leaped in his chest, and his body tingled with excitement.

Marko stood there also, fear evident in his eyes. Or was it the reflection of his own fright that Cveja saw? The moment of truth had arrived. Cveja felt eager, yet resigned. This was his last chance.

"Now remember my instructions," Hans said. He struck out ahead, his tall figure slightly bent. When they heard the loud, melodious sound of a nightingale twice, they followed. It was his signal. In single file the three men moved silently forward like phantom figures in the night, stepping cautiously, noiselessly. They hiked across rolling meadows, through shrouded stands of trees, past fields of barley and oats. They walked on the road and through the fields. In the eerie silence, they strained to discern any hint of sound.

Out of nowhere, a motor suddenly growled. A vehicle was approaching. The guide pulled Cveja and Marko behind some tall bushes that grew beside the road, and they dropped to the ground. Lying there flat on their stomachs, their nostrils filled with the musty scent of the soil. The whirring motor grew louder as a jeep approached. The noise heightened, then died down and disappeared. When the guide got up, the two men followed, trusting his instincts, and continued on their journey.

After traveling for more than two hours, Cveja estimated they must have covered about six miles. The guide turned into a stand of pine trees, stopped, and faced them. "In about 30 minutes we'll reach 'no man's land,' " he said, "the most dangerous part of the trip." He turned toward Cveja and stepped closer. "How can I be sure you're not a spy? How do I know you won't betray me to the border guards?" The whites of his eyes and a gold tooth in his mouth gleamed in the darkness, reflecting the moonlight leaking through the clouds. "I can tell you right now you won't succeed." Reaching under his oversized jacket, he pulled out two guns, one in each hand. "This revolver is for you and me." He shoved it into Cveja's mid-section. "The other one is for the border guards. They won't take me alive—or you either, for that matter."

Cveja swallowed hard, his mind working frantically. What had happened to the gentle, genial man who had fed them, sheltered them, and instructed them? What words would convince this man of his sincerity? What could he say that he had not already said? After all he had endured, was this how his life would end? Had God brought him this far only to let him die on the threshold of freedom? Cveja breathed a quick prayer heavenward and felt a sudden, unnatural calm. In quiet resignation he spoke.

"Sir, everything I told you is true. I'm not a Communist, much less a spy. I'm a Christian. God is my judge. If you don't believe me, there's nothing more I can say." He shrugged, "You might as well kill me right now."

For a long, terror-filled minute, the man locked eyes with Cveja. At last he relaxed. "I *do* believe you," he said, his voice returning to normal again. He slipped the revolvers back into the holsters under his jacket. Cveja breathed freely once more. The pounding in his chest subsided, but his legs threatened to give way. Marko went limp.

"I'm sorry I had to do this," Hans said apologetically. "But in this work I can't afford to take chances." He patted the sides of his jacket. "I sleep with these guns. My life is always in danger. If the police ever come after me, they'll regret it," he sighed.

"You can pay me now," he said, his voice taking on a cheerful tone. "I didn't take your money earlier because I needed to be sure. We're almost to the border now."

Cveja pulled out the 60,000 dinars he had saved for this purpose and gave them to the man. Marko did the same. Hans counted the bills and stuffed them in a zippered pocket in his pant leg. "OK, now back to work," he said matter-of-factly.

He pointed to an open area of tall grass on the other side of the stand of trees. "That field is mined. We'll have to crawl through it for half a mile. I'll go in front. When I signal, follow in single file. Don't veer left or right." Marko and Cveja glanced at each other and nodded numbly.

Hans went on ahead, cutting a narrow swath through the grass as he hugged the ground. When they heard the call of the nightingale twice, Marko and Cveja followed as directed, their knees and elbows digging into the earth as they pulled themselves along on their stomachs. Now and again they stopped to rest or watch and listen. At last they stopped about 50 yards from an embankment about 18 feet high which leveled off at the top.

The guide gestured toward it without saying a word. *So this is no man's land,* Cveja thought. The three men pressed close to the ground, bodies taut, heads down. Blades of dewy grass brushed their faces. They could hear each other's shallow breathing as they listened intently for signs of the guards.

Soon they heard distant footfalls crackling on the gravel path atop the embankment. The sound was coming from both directions and gradually grew louder. Two guards met on the path almost directly ahead of them. "*Zdravo, druže* [Greetings, comrade]," the muffled greetings floated down to the men hiding below. The guards conversed briefly, and then their footsteps crackled again on the gravel and faded away.

When all was quiet, the guide nodded toward a light off the elevated path to the right. A small wooden structure, a *karaula,* was built into the embankment. It was almost undetectable in the dark except for the dim light that sifted through a small round window.

Every two hours they change shifts. They take a break and go into the karaula for a drink or smoke and to report to their replacements. During that brief interval the border is unguarded. That's when we move. We have only ten minutes to cross. When I say, 'Now!' run like the devil and don't stop! The guide's words echoed in Cveja's mind.

Stretched out on the ground, the three men waited, barely breathing. Then a hoarse voice whispered: "Now!" In a flash, the guide jumped up. He grabbed both men by the arms, pulled them to their feet, and then dashed toward the embankment. Cveja ran closely behind, panicked and panting. It was now or never. The ridged soles of his boots gripped the ground as he began to climb.

Nearing the top, he suddenly became aware of the absence of sound behind him—he could not hear Marko's footsteps or heavy breathing. An anxious glance over his shoulder revealed his companion struggling at the base of the grassy slope, his smooth-soled shoes slipping on the slick grass. He had not made any headway.

Cveja scrambled back down, his mind and body working feverishly. At any moment the guards would come out and bullets would fly. Grabbing Marko by his arm and jacket, he yanked and tugged. Marko tried to get traction on the slope but kept slipping back.

Cveja got behind him and pushed, his shoes digging into the ground. Marko was taller and heavier, and Cveja summoned all his strength. A clump of dirt and grass broke off beneath his feet, and Cveja slipped back. Desperate now, he pushed like a madman wild with fear. He had to get this man to the top. Somehow he prevailed. When they reached the top of the embankment, he let go. "Hurry, Marko!" Cveja whispered and sprinted ahead.

"I . . . I can't," Marko groaned. Cveja looked back again. Marko was stooped over, knees bent, feet dragging, paralyzed with fear. Again Cveja turned back, delirious with fright.

"Come on, Marko, move!" he urged. Cveja grabbed him under the arm and jerked him forward. There at the top of the embankment, the gravel road gave them traction. But time was fast running out.

Suddenly they heard a rumble off to the right. Cveja turned to see two shafts of light piercing the night sky. The patrol jeep was ascending a rise in the road, heading straight toward them. In a second the road would level off, and the headlights would flood over them. Terrified, Cveja gave Marko one last fierce shove that hurled him over the edge of the embankment. Cveja dove after him.

Tumbling down the other side into the ditch, Cveja heard Marko bounce from tree to tree. Then all went silent. A second later the jeep rumbled noisily past them.

Cveja got up and looked around. In the subsequent silence, he feared that his companion had been injured. "Marko, are you alive?" he called softly.

"I think so," came the uncertain reply. Marko stood up, rubbing his shoulder and side.

Both men were bruised and sore. But where was their guide? Looking around, they saw the outline of his figure several yards away and stumbled toward it.

"Whew! That was close," Hans said. "Come here." He pointed to what looked like a white tombstone. "This is a border marker," he said. "On one side it says 'Jugoslavija' and on the other, 'Österreich.'" They looked in awe at the large engraved letters and stepped over to the Austrian side.

"You are now in a free country," their guide said, smiling. "God bless you and good luck." He hugged the two men and kissed them on both cheeks. "I must get back before dawn." Then he ran back toward the place from which they had come. Cveja and Marko watched him until he disappeared.

CHAPTER 10

DANGERS AT THE BORDER

*B*e careful at the border. The Yugoslav border patrol can cross over into Austria and kidnap you. And watch out for border pockets. You may think you're in Austria when you've actually wound back into Yugoslavia. The guide's words replayed in Cveja's mind now as he and Marko debated over the exact direction in which to proceed. It was still dark, and the terrain on the Austrian side rose steeply. Rocks and forests abounded, and mountains loomed black and desolate.

"We need to go in that direction," Cveja said, pointing toward the north.

"I don't think so, Cveja. We need to go *that* way," Marko countered, pointing farther east.

Cveja shook his head. "The three borders converge here," he said. "If we go the way you want, Marko, we'll end up in Hungary."

"No, Cveja, you're wrong," Marko insisted.

"OK, OK. We'll go your way. But I'm telling you, Marko, you'll see that I'm right." The two men started off. They had not gone far when, in the pre-dawn darkness, they noticed something in the distance.

"What is that?" Marko squinted, trying to make out the form. "It looks like some kind of frame . . . or maybe a fence."

"It *is* a fence," Cveja replied. As they walked closer they made out wooden posts and steel wires strung horizontally between the posts.

"But what's that strange black object hanging on it?" Marko stared ahead.

"That looks like . . . it is! It's a body, a charred body!" Cveja gasped, recoiling at the sight. "That's an electrified fence at the Hungarian border! The poor soul was trying to escape."

Horrified, the two men quickly made an abrupt U-turn and retraced their steps. Walking along in silence, the image haunted them, a reminder of the prevalent dangers at the border they had escaped. Minutes later, Cveja spoke. "We're going the right way now. Trust me, Marko, we'll be all right. My sense of direction hasn't failed me yet." Under his breath he prayed, "Please, God, let it not fail me now. Thank You for protecting us thus far."

Trudging through a thicket of pine trees, their weary feet sank into patches of pine needles, and their nostrils filled with the fresh fragrance. Cveja sensed a change in the atmosphere—an overwhelming excitement had replaced the apprehension and dread. A strange new feeling of freedom rushed through his veins.

Inhaling deeply, Cveja thought the chilly night air smelled fresher and sweeter on this side of the border; that people who breathe free air must feel different. He was one of them now, and the joy flooding his being washed away the weariness and energized his stride. All the disappointments and reversals of the past two months faded away in the success of his escape. He had finally beaten the border.

Soon they came to a road, and they turned west to follow it. Giddy with joy, they walked on. Before long the night began to wash out of the sky, and the yellow sun peeked over the horizon. The countryside stirred to life. Roosters crowed their greetings to the new day. Morning birds burst into joyful melodies. Here and there a dog yapped. Somewhere in the meadows, cows mooed, their bells tinkling.

A light came on in an old farmhouse as they passed by, and the faint odor of wood smoke from a nearby chimney wafted toward them. Before long the bright beams of the rising sun gilded the mountain ridges and filled the meadows, like a blessing from heaven to the weary travelers on their first day of freedom.

They had not gone very far before a vehicle appeared over the rise in the road ahead. The police jeep, identifiable by the Gendarmerie-Polizei license plate, stopped at the side of the road just ahead of them. Two policemen inside raised their hands and gestured toward the two travelers. "*Gruss Gott* [Greetings in the Lord]!" they said politely in the soft German dialect spoken in Austria. "Are you refugees?"

"*Ja, wir sind* [Yes, we are]," Cveja replied in German.

"There's a bus that goes to Jennersdorf, to the refugee camp. We can take you to it so you don't have to walk," they offered, still speaking in German.

"Which way is Jennersdorf?" Cveja asked.

They pointed behind them in the direction Cveja and Marko were walking. "Keep going that way. But it's pretty far."

"*Danke* [Thanks]," we'll walk," he told them.

Without stopping, the two travelers continued on. Getting into a strange car so close to the border, even a police vehicle in a free country, was risky. They had come to distrust police in their own land and were not too sure these police were any different.

Not long afterward, a farm wagon drove up behind them. It passed and then pulled over to the side. This time there were two men in work clothes. "Do you need a ride?" they called out in German, turning around.

If they offer you a ride, don't trust them. They'll demand your money. If you have none, they'll turn you over to the border patrol for a reward. The guide's warning shouted in Cveja's head.

"*Nein, vielen dank* [No, thanks very much]!" Cveja called back. Out of the corner of his mouth, he whispered to Marko. "Whatever I tell you, agree. Repeat, '*Ja, dass stimmt doch* [Yes, that's right].' " And so as they continued walking past the wagon, Cveja talked in German to Marko, who didn't understand a word. "*Und wenn des Buben . . .* [And when the children . . .]" Cveja began, making up a story.

"*Ja, dass stimmt doch,*" Marko repeated as soon as Cveja paused. He spoke loud enough for the men in the wagon to hear.

"*Kein Glück* [No luck]," Cveja overheard one of the men behind him say. Then the motor revved up, and the men drove past them. Cveja watched the wagon lumber down the road.

"It worked!" Marko blurted out happily.

"*Jawohl, mein Herr Marko* [Of course, Mr. Marko]. We're on our way to work our fields!" Cveja joked.

"*Ja, dass stimmt doch,*" Marko mocked agreement. They could laugh now and did so with gusto. The feared border that had swallowed up so many lives had been cheated of its prey this time.

It was late morning when the two wanderers arrived in Jennersdorf, a small town about eight miles from the border and far from any city. A sign off the main road reading "Fluchtlinge Lager" pointed the way to the refugee camp. Following the tree-lined road, they came to a high stone-wall enclosure. A guard stood next to the massive iron gate that spanned the 10-foot-wide entrance. He nodded to them and swung open one wing of the huge gate. Stepping into the cobblestone courtyard, they gasped in amazement.

"*This* is a refugee camp?" Marko asked incredulously. On their left stood an attractive cream-colored, two-story mansion boasting a red corrugated tile roof. At the rear of the courtyard, an L-shaped, one-story building extended from the mansion and turned sharply to border the right side of the courtyard. A covered, colonnaded corridor provided shade along the front of this building, and there were several doors spaced at regular intervals along its walls. In the center of the open courtyard, two men stood talking beside an unused, sculptured, concrete fountain.

"This must have been a beautiful residence once, probably belonging to a count," Cveja exclaimed as he surveyed their new surroundings appreciatively.

Smiling at their astonished expressions, the guard directed them to an office on the ground floor of the mansion. Exhausted, grimy, and famished, they entered eagerly. The nameplate on the desk read "Herman Müller, Director."

From behind his desk, Mr. Müller (MEW-ler) looked them over and then asked matter of factly, "What are your names?" He took out two forms and prepared to write. The men replied with their full names.

"You are Serbs, is that correct?" he continued, recording their answers. "Serbian Orthodox, I presume?"

"No, we're Protestants—Seventh-day Adventists," Cveja said. The director looked up, appearing somewhat surprised.

"Did you know you have a church in Salzburg?" he asked. "I know about it because the pastor there has helped a lot of refugees. Different organizations offer assistance to different groups. Catholic Charities helps Catholics and the World Council of Churches helps everyone else."

"That's good to know," Cveja replied. "Thank you."

"Can you tell me how you escaped?" the man asked, returning to his paper work.

"We had a guide," Cveja answered. "He took us across the border from Slovenia." Even as he spoke, he wondered how much information to divulge.

As if reading his mind, Müller remarked, "Whatever you tell me now we will verify." He recorded the rest of the information the two men gave him.

When he finished writing, he looked up. "As soon as I confirm the accuracy of this information, I'll let you know if you qualify for political asylum. It should take no more than a week. If you do, you'll be free to go anywhere in Austria. You could even stay here temporarily if your papers are in order." He stood up while continuing his speech. "On the other hand, if our information indicates that you are economic rather than political refugees, you will be deported." He spoke the words lightly, casually, and detached—like a message repeated mindlessly day after day. But to the desperate refugees who heard these words, they meant the difference between life and death.

"I'll show you where you can stay until your cases are decided. Come with me." He led them out the door and across the courtyard to a room that contained three beds. "The water closet and shower room are in the hallway. The cafeteria is in the main building. If you hurry, you can still get lunch." Eyeing their soiled clothes he offered, "If you need a change of clothing, come back to my office. Oh, and by the way, we lock the gates at 11:00 p.m. That's for your own protection."

"How can that guy verify this kind of information?" Marko asked Cveja over lunch in the nearly empty cafeteria. Most of the refugees had already eaten.

"Maybe some of it," Cveja replied, "but I think his main source for verification is his eyes. He's watching us."

After lunch the two men showered and changed into the clean, used clothing which the director had given them. Finding a large portable aluminum tub near a water pump on a table outside their door, they laundered their own clothes. Then they hung them out to dry on a rope strung between two oak trees behind their room. That night when they retired, they were asleep before their heads hit their pillows. It was the first comfortable bed they had slept in for days.

Early the next morning, sounds from the courtyard woke Cveja. He quietly dressed and stepped out into the early morning mist. Sauntering into the deserted courtyard, he watched the guard unlock the big iron gate. It was 6:00 a.m. and still dark.

When he returned to the room, he found Marko up and dressed. A little while later they filed into the cafeteria for breakfast along with the other refugees, mostly young people from the Communist countries of Hungary and Yugoslavia. Cveja counted 50 people in all. A staffer called the roll. When he finished, the man made an announcement.

"If any of you wish to earn some money, there is a job for you at the railroad station. A trainload of coal has arrived. Workers are needed to unload it." Five hands, including Cveja's, shot up. With the immediate needs of shelter and food supplied so generously by the Austrian government, it was easy for refugees to feel that they didn't need to do anything to help themselves. But Cveja had no intention of remaining in the refugee camp for long.

At the railroad station, those who had responded were each given a shovel and directed to a loaded freight train, each man assigned to a car. In the absence of gloves, Cveja wore an extra pair of socks on his hands to protect them. After all he was unaccustomed to hard physical labor. As soon as he filled the bin beside the car, someone wheeled it away and brought an empty bin for him to fill. And so went the day.

Cveja worked 10-hour days on Thursday, Friday, and Monday, a marathon attested to by the blisters on his hands. On Tuesday, he received 500 schillings as payment—100 for each car he had emptied. To his delight, the money exceeded the 230 schillings he needed for train fare to Salzburg. He sent 100 schillings in a letter to Voja in Italy and kept the rest.

The following day was Wednesday, September 18, one week from the day Cveja arrived at the camp. As Cveja walked across the courtyard that morning, an unusually cheerful Müller called him into his office.

"Congratulations!" he said. "I think you're waiting for this paper." Smiling, he held out an envelope. Cveja read the letter inside and grinned. It was the notice of political asylum.

"Thank you so much, Mr. Müller," Cveja said. "Now that I have this, I'll be leaving as soon as I return these clothes you loaned me."

"As you wish," the director replied. "Remember, once you leave the camp, we can't help you. You're on your own." Cveja turned to go.

"Oh, by the way, it was good to hear that you shoveled coal at the railroad station," he added. "So many refugees feel they are entitled to government aid because they fought for their freedom."

"Thank you," Cveja said again and left.

Back in his room, he told Marko his news. His companion had not yet received his notice and would have to wait. Cveja changed into his own freshly laundered clothing, returned the borrowed clothes to the office, and bid Marko and Mr. Müller goodbye. Then he walked to the train station and boarded the next train to Salzburg.

As the electric train slid out of the station and plunged into more mountainous terrain, he wondered what problems might lay ahead. By the time the train arrived in Salzburg, it would be night. The only place he knew to go was the Seventh-day Adventist church. Someone in the camp had given him the address, and he pulled out the slip of paper from his pocket on which he had jotted it down. Traditionally, churches held mid-week prayer services on Wednesday evenings. If he got there in time, he could ask one of the members for help. If the church was closed, he didn't know where he would go. A quick glance at his watch told him it was already getting late.

Left: Belgrade's Kalemegdan Park is shown with the Messenger of Victory Memorial on the upper terrace. It was here that Voja told Cveja his name was on the approved list for a tour group to Rome.

Right: When the family posed for this picture, they did not know that soon their lives would change drastically. This is the last picture taken just before Voja left for Rome. Shown back row left to right are: Cveja, Vera, and Voja. Their mother Mara, little Jovica, and Nata are in the front. Mica had not yet been released from prison.

Below: This map of the former Yugoslavia shows the six republics comprising it at the time of this story and before Yugoslavia broke apart in the 1990s. Some of the cities mentioned in the story are indicated.

Above: During his five months in Rome, Voja visited the sights. Here he stands on the roof of St. Peter's Church, whose construction and history he had related to the tour group before disappearing.

Left: Voja and Cveja are shown with their Austrian friend Adolf, whose ministerial credentials helped Cveja rescue friends from a refugee camp from which refugees were mysteriously disappearing.

Above: After escaping to Austria, Cveja organized a choir composed of Yugoslav refugees who sang in Serbo-Croatian to the German-speaking congregation in Salzburg. Here Cveja directs while Voja (back row right) sings with the group.

Right: Voja and Cveja pose with the Hohensalzburg Fortress of Salzburg in the background.

Right: When Voja received a religious brochure with a picture of a young lady on the cover, he cut it out and told friends she was his girlfriend in America. Since no one knew her name, they called her by the title on the brochure, "The Unpardonable Sin."

Left: While on a visit to Paris for their friend's wedding, the twins visited the Eiffel Tower.

Below: Kafa and Djoka, the happy wedded pair (center) stand on the steps of the Paris Adventist Church flanked by the groom's family (behind them), members of the wedding party (Cveja front left and Voja second from right), as well as many church friends.

Right: After someone maliciously accused Voja of being a communist spy, a series of astounding events resulted in good news. Voja could smile again with the Consul in front of the American Consulate building.

Above: On their last day in Austria, the twins posed with a third refugee who, with them, occupied the last three available seats on the Pan American refugee flight to New York City. In the background one of the two Mercedes refugee buses waits to take them to the airport in Munich.

Below: Mladen and Mela pose with their four children at the time: Mirjana and Nevenka, born in Yugoslavia, and little Nadica and Djordje, who were born in New York City. The family shared their small apartment with the twins until they could rent their own place.

Above: Cveja and Voja are shown here at their first job in the United States. One of the plans they worked on in this office was the Turkish Embassy which required a knowledge of French, German, Italian, as well as the Metric System.

Left: The first Sabbath at the Yugoslavian Church in New York City, Voja met Ann, a.k.a., "The Unpardonable Sin." Here they are shown during their courting days.

Right: Eight months after arriving on American shores, Voja and Ann were married in the Yugoslavian Church. They are shown here on their wedding day, August 16, 1959.

Left: One year after Voja and Ann married, Cveja and Diana tied the knot. This picture shows the two couples on that happy day.

Left: As soon as Voja became an American citizen, he began the process to bring his mother to America. Here mother Mara is shown celebrating one of her birthdays in America.

Above: Nata, Jovica, and Mi*f*a stand in the Customs and Immigration area at New York's Idlewild International Airport after landing in America. They are photographed from the upper floor where family members waited to welcome them.

Above: After settling into their apartment, Nata, Jovica, and Mica look happy to be finally living in America.

Right: On a trip to Europe in 1961, Voja introduced Ann to his three Serbian friends in Salzburg. Ratko and Boba (left of the couple) and Duško (right), stand in front of one of Salzburg's many confectionery shops.

Left: At Idlewild Airport, the family welcomed Vera for one of several visits. Shown left to right are: Voja, Jovica, Mother Mara, Nata, Cveja, Diana (Cveja's wife at the time).

Right: Diana and Ann dressed in authentic Serbian folk costumes for an international fair in New York City. They wear the century-old handmade *libada* jackets that Mara had hidden underground from the Nazis to preserve them for her future daughters-in-law.

Above: Here the twins reunite with friends Elizabeth (center, holding daughter Esther) and husband Djordje (extreme right). Also shown (left to right) are: Ann, Voja, Cveja, Nata, Diana, and (front row) Djurdja (Elizabeth's and Djordje's daughter) and Jovica (Nata's son). Elizabeth and Djordje had escaped from Yugoslavia earlier and took Voja in when he defected from his tour group in Rome.

Above: Ann and Voja are shown with their son George.

Above: The twins' children pose together in a New York park. Maria and Johnny (left) and Danny, the eldest (extreme right), are Cveja's and Diana's children. George (second from right) is Voja's and Ann's son.

Right: Maria, Cveja's and Diana's middle child, and George, Voja's and Ann's only child, pose in Serbian folk costumes for a special occasion. The cousins are just three weeks apart in age.

Below: Choir director Cveja stands at the pulpit with the Jackson Church choir behind him. The church building had formerly been a Jewish synagogue and Voja re-designed and renovated the sanctuary and the building to accommodate a church school on the third floor. Cveja worked with him.

CHAPTER 11

THE SINGING STRANGER

At the side of the tall entrance doors, a brass plate gleamed in the light from the street lamp. "Seventh-day Adventist Church and Salzburg Conference," Cveja read, standing in front of the attractive five-story building on Franz Josef Strasse. He tried the door, and it opened. As he stepped inside he let out a sigh of relief.

It was 9:00 p.m., too late for prayer meeting, but he heard singing. Evidently there were people still in the building. His tension eased. *"Und ich, Johannes, sah die Heilige Stadt. . . .* [And I, John, saw the Holy City. . . .]" The joyous strains of the Bach melody rose up like incense from the basement. He spied a staircase and followed the sounds down to a room with the door ajar.

Peering into the large room, he saw a group of singers on the platform at one end of the room. A slim young man stood in front of them, directing what appeared to be the church choir.

Although he entered quietly, all eyes turned toward the stranger who had suddenly appeared. The choir director stopped and glanced over his shoulder. Cveja smiled shyly and shifted his pants. He cleared his throat and strode toward the director.

"I know that song," Cveja told the young man in German. Then he stretched out his arms, filled his lungs, and opened his mouth. His resonant tenor voice continued the melody. The director's face beamed his appreciation.

"Won't you please join us?" he invited graciously, motioning Cveja toward the tenor section. The men in the back row shuffled over to make a space for him, and the choir continued their practice.

While they sang, a short, rotund man dressed in a suit and tie entered the room and stood beside the door with his hands behind his back. A blissful smile played on his round face as he stood listening with his eyes closed.

When an unfamiliar tenor voice rose above the chorus his eyes popped open, and he spied the stranger. At the end of practice, as choir members surrounded and welcomed Cveja, the man approached.

"My name is Hugo Schnötzinger [SHNET-zing-er]." He smiled and extended his hand. "I'm the pastor of the church here."

"Svetozar Vitorovic," Cveja gave his full name. "I just came from Jennersdorf."

"Oh, I see," the pastor said, nodding. His voice betrayed a tone Cveja could not at once identify. The two men were conversing when Cveja suddenly noticed the choir members leaving and felt a surge of urgency. It was getting late, and he had no place to spend the night. "I need a place to stay tonight, Pastor Schnötzinger," he said. "Do you know where I might find a room?"

The pastor paused and then beckoned. "Come with me," he said. Cveja followed him up the stairs to his first floor office. Inside he motioned Cveja toward a chair, then sat down behind the walnut desk and leaned back in his high office chair, his hands gripping the arms.

Too nervous to sit, Cveja paced. Back and forth in the small space he walked, his eyes focused on the floor. Without even looking up, he sensed the pastor's scrutinizing stare. He suddenly became aware that he must look like any of the other refugees who had fled their homes with only the clothes on their backs.

"Tell me, young man, how did you come to be here?" the pastor asked.

"Someone at Jennersdorf gave me the church's address," he said, still pacing. "I escaped from Yugoslavia and spent the last week at the refugee camp. This morning I received my political asylum and took the train here." He paused.

"The camp was too close to the border, and I was afraid to stay there. Someone could easily turn me over to the border patrol." He stopped and faced the pastor. "I shoveled coal for three days to earn some money for train fare. You can still see the blisters." He looked at his hands and extended them, palms up, toward the pastor.

"Hmmm, yes, I like a man who isn't afraid of hard work!" Schnötzinger said. He smiled and leaned forward to look at Cveja's hands. Pleased, he settled back in his chair. "Tell me more about yourself."

Cveja shifted his trousers and resumed pacing. He fidgeted anxiously as he spoke. "I'm an architect. I left my mother and sisters in Yugoslavia. My twin brother is in Rome. He and I were very active in the Belgrade church. I directed the youth choir, and he led the youth mandolin orchestra. I'm hoping he can come here eventually."

The pastor narrowed his deep-set eyes and let out an audible sigh. "So many refugees, so many grand stories. Everybody was a big shot in his own country," he said with a sarcastic gesture. "Then they come here, and I find out they're small people." He grunted and clasped his hands.

"Three weeks ago a man came to me. He claimed he was a pastor in Yugoslavia. I believed him and gave him a room." He raised his hands and shrugged. "A few days later I discovered supplies missing from the boiler room—an electric saw and some other equipment—expensive stuff. So I went to the post office right away. Luckily they still had the package. He had brought it in that morning to mail to Yugoslavia. I told them my suspicions, and they let me open it. Inside I found the missing equipment. Of course, I had to ask the man to leave."

"I understand, Pastor Schnötzinger. But I can only speak for myself," Cveja replied meekly, beginning to feel uncomfortable.

"So how do I know you're telling me the truth? Why should I trust you?" the pastor asked. The directness of his words startled Cveja. This man had the power to help or turn him away, and Cveja had nowhere else to go. In Jennersdorf he had exchanged the US$20 bill wedged between the treads of his hiking boots for 500 schillings. Combined with his earnings from shoveling coal, and after buying the train ticket and sending his brother 100 schillings, he had only 670 schillings left.

"Didn't you have a man named Laza Kramar here, and his wife, Sida?" Cveja asked. "They're good friends of mine from Yugoslavia."

"You know Laza?" the pastor asked. His voice took on a cheerful tone. "They were fine people, very fine." He paused. "Do you happen to know Anton Lorencin?"

"Pastor Lorencin? Why yes. Quite well, in fact," Cveja replied. "He's president of the Yugoslavian Church Union."

Pastor Schnötzinger looked satisfied. Nevertheless, he waved his finger. "Let me make myself clear, Brother Vitorovic. I play my cards on top of the table." He placed his hands palms down on the desk with a thud and then pointed to Cveja. "You could be my son. You have an excellent voice, and you could be an asset to our church." He rose to his feet and came around the desk. "It's late now. Yes, you may stay here tonight. But tomorrow we'll talk more."

The pastor led Cveja up the stairs to the third floor. As they walked down the long hallway, he pointed to the different doors. "This is a dormitory room for Bible workers passing through; two ladies occupy it now," he said. "There's one water closet on this floor for men and another for women. The divided shower room is shared by the residents on this floor. And this studio apartment is rented to a young intern pastor about your age. You'll probably meet him tomorrow. I think you'll like him." He went a little farther and stopped at a door, put a key in the lock, and pushed it open. "This studio apartment is vacant. The bed is clean. I hope you enjoy your sleep."

Cveja shook the pastor's hand and thanked him.

"I live upstairs with my family," the pastor said before leaving. "I'll see you tomorrow morning."

As soon as the pastor closed the door, Cveja collapsed into bed. When he awoke the next morning, light was filtering into the room from both the window and the windowed door that opened onto the balcony. For one anxious moment, he could not remember where he was, and he wondered whether he had dreamed the events of the day before and the previous week.

Sitting up, he surveyed his new surroundings. Besides the large bed, the room contained two night stands, an armoire, a small table, two chairs, and a metal stove-sink-cabinet combination with a mirror above it. On the north side of the building, a pantry with a concrete floor kept food cold. *I could live like this*, he thought to himself.

He ventured out onto the balcony to take a peek at the view. Clouds covered the mountains but from an angle he could see the street below from an angle and the railroad station not far away.

Refreshed and eager, he washed up, dressed, and prepared to start searching for a job. Since he knew both the German language and the metric system, he hoped he'd have no problem. As he finished dressing, a knock sounded at the door.

"Pastor Schnötzinger would like to see you," a lady's voice called.

"I'm the pastor's secretary," the attractive young lady explained when

Cveja opened the door. He followed her down to the pastor's office where a ruddy-complexioned, balding young man sat. He appeared to be about the same age as Cveja.

"This is your countryman, Pastor Adolf Kinder," Pastor Schnötzinger said. "He's the one I told you about last night who has an apartment on your floor. He's German, born in Yugoslavia—a Volksdeutscher. Speaks Serbo-Croatian, like you."

Adolf extended his hand toward Cveja. "I was 14 when my family and I escaped from Yugoslavia. That was before the communists came," Adolf said. "You'll have to tell me more about yourself."

Cveja smiled as he shook hands with the young pastor. "I'm sure I'll have time," he replied as he sat down.

Pastor Schnötzinger continued. "Last night I mentioned some bad experiences I've had because I trusted people." He pursed his lips and shrugged his shoulders. "I have learned now to ask refugees for references." His smile faded, and he looked at Cveja questioningly. "You said you know Pastor Lorencin. Is that correct? I'm going to call him right now." As he dialed the long-distance operator, his eyes never left Cveja's face.

"Person-to-person, please."

Cveja felt his face flush. He had not confided in Pastor Lorencin his plans to escape, and he wondered what the pastor would say.

"Pastor Lorencin here." Cveja's keen ears picked up the familiar, modulated voice on the other end. Pastor Schnötzinger had seated him close to his desk so he could hear.

"This is your Austrian brother, Pastor Schnötzinger," he said, speaking in German. "I have a young man sitting in my office, a Brother Vitorovic. He says he knows you." His eyes still on Cveja, he repeated what Cveja had told him.

There was silence on the other end for a moment. "You say Brother Vitorovic is there?" Cveja heard the voice escalate in pitch. "Which one?"

"Svetozar."

"Svetozar. Thank God! We thought he was dead." There was a pause. "Yes, what he says is true. I know him well. Is Vojislav there also?"

"No. I understand he's in Italy."

"Well, *Bruder* Schnötzinger, we were sorry to lose these two young men.

Apparently our loss is your gain. I'm sure his brother will find a way to join him. You'll enjoy them both."

There was a broad grin on the pastor's face when he hung up the receiver and came around his desk to the front. "*Willkommen*, Brother Vitorovic!" he boomed, enveloping Cveja in a bear hug. "Pastor Lorencin had only good things to say about you. I will rent you an apartment, but it will have to be conditional, you understand—if there are no problems. And if your brother comes here, he can stay with you." Reaching again for the phone he exclaimed, "Yes, and I will do even more—I will help you find a job."

CHAPTER 12

SURPRISES IN SALZBURG

Twenty minutes later, Cveja and Adolf were still visiting in the pastor's office when Walter arrived. "This is Brother Svetozar Vitorovic," the pastor said, introducing the two men. "I'd like you to help him find a job."

"Vitorovic?" Walter exclaimed. He turned to face Cveja, his mouth hanging open and his eyes wide with surprise. "Svetozar Vitorovic?"

Cveja nodded.

"Das ist unglaublich [That is unbelievable]!" he almost shouted, unable to contain himself. "Your sister Nata is a guest in my house right now!"

"My Nata?" Cveja gasped, and his hand flew to his chest as if to still his fluttering heart. He had lost all contact with home in recent days and could not believe his ears.

"Yes, *your* Nata. Your sister!" Walter laughed. "Nata and I have known each other since we went to Missionary School together in Zagreb. That was almost 20 years ago, you know," he continued in high spirits. "I know you, too, Cveja. At least, I feel like I do. Nata talks about her brothers all the time." He put his hand on Cveja's shoulder. "Why, of course I'll help you find a job. But first I must take you to see Nata."

Walter took Cveja by the arm and led him outside to his Volkswagen Beetle. On the way to the man's home, they talked eagerly. "How long has Nata been here? I can't believe it," Cveja said.

"Three weeks already. Next week her visitor visa expires," Walter paused, his face sobering. "She's been anxiously waiting for Mica to escape so they could apply to go to America. With his history, it would be easy. But if he doesn't make it by next week, she'll have to go back." He shook his head.

"Oh, I can't wait to see her! My dear Nata," Cveja exclaimed. "Is she well?"

"Oh, yes, but very worried. Rumors said you were dead, but she refused to believe them. I'm anxious to see the expression on her face when she sees you very much alive!" Walter chuckled.

"The secret police were after me. I couldn't write home," Cveja explained. "It's a long, long story."

Walter looked at him. "I can't imagine what that's like—having to escape and all that," he said sympathetically.

They drove down a narrow street and stopped in front of a modest house. "This is it. My palace," Walter said, opening the door to get out.

When Cveja climbed out of the car, the front door flew open. Nata had been looking out the window and had seen the car arrive. The moment she caught sight of Cveja, she dashed out of the house, crying and laughing. She could not contain her joy and talked and laughed through the tears streaming down her face.

"Cveja, Cveja, my brother Cveja! You *are* alive! I knew it. I knew God would protect you!" She wrapped him in a fierce embrace and held him for a long time. Walter watched nearby, his eyes watering.

"Nata, how did the government let you out?" Cveja asked after they had wiped away all the tears and turned to go into the house.

"Walter and Hilde sent me a letter inviting me to visit them—an affidavit of support as they call it. I applied for a passport and a visitor's visa, and . . . I don't know . . . they gave them to me!" She shrugged, giggling, then grew serious. "Mica was supposed to escape with Jovica while I'm still here. A friend promised to help him." She wrung her hands in anguish, her eyes brimming with tears again. "I'll have to go back next week. I'm a bundle of nerves, missing Jovica, waiting for Mica to escape. What will I do, Cveja?" The tears flowed freely, spilling down her cheeks as she sobbed deeply. "Every time I see a child I think of Jovica and break down," she sniffled, wiping her eyes.

"I know, Nata. I understand," Cveja said, thinking of his brother and feeling the empty ache inside. He put a comforting arm around his sister's shoulder. "And Mother? How is she?" he asked, changing the subject.

"I left her in Šabac with Vera. She and Duja (DOO-ya) will take care of her," Nata replied. "Wait until I let them know you're here!" Her face brightened. "They've been worried too." She looked lovingly at her brother.

"You are well, and my heart is full. It must have been awful for you, Cveja. You've been gone so long."

He nodded. "I wouldn't want to go through it again. But the worst is over now, thank God."

After Nata and Cveja caught up on family news, Walter returned to the room carrying a newspaper in his hand. He had left the two alone for several minutes so they could talk in private. Now the conversation turned to Cveja's search for a job. Sitting beside Cveja on the sofa, Walter leafed through the paper to the jobs section and ran his finger down the column of want ads.

"Here's something." His finger stopped halfway down the page. "Wagner Construction Company. They're looking for a construction manager to visit job sites." Lifting his head, he turned to Cveja. "This doesn't require an architect, but you could probably do the job. Wagner is a large company with an excellent reputation."

Cveja craned his neck to read the ad for himself. He scratched his head. "A possibility, maybe. . . . Are there any architectural firms in town?"

"A few. I don't know much about them." Walter returned to the paper. "Well, look at this. Just what you're looking for." He pointed to another ad farther down the column. "Robert Schäfer [SHAY-fer] is looking for a qualified architect." He looked up from the paper, thinking out loud, "Schäfer, Schäfer . . . I've heard of him. He's a good architect himself."

It was still early in the day, so Cveja called the companies in the ads and made appointments at both—Wagner Construction later that day and Robert Schäfer the next morning.

"Yes, we can give you the job of construction manager, Herr Vitorovic," Wagner's general manager said after an hour-long interview later that afternoon.

Cveja hesitated. The salary and benefits offered were excellent, but he wanted to check out the other job. He'd prefer to work as an architect.

The general manager seemed to notice his hesitation. "Think about it if you'd like. Let me know your decision by noon tomorrow," he added. With the interview over, Cveja and Walter returned home.

As soon as they parked in front of the house, the door swung open. Nata stood in the doorway beaming, still basking in her brother's presence. "What happened? Did you have any luck? Did you get the job?" she inquired as they entered the house.

"Wagner offered it to me," Cveja replied, grinning, "but I'd rather work in an architectural firm. I'll decide after my appointment with Schäfer in the morning."

At 10:00 a.m. the next day, Walter and Cveja arrived at Robert Schäfer's house in an attractive suburb of Salzburg called Elsbethen. The architect's gray stucco house fronted the Salzach River and occupied the entire cul-de-sac. The house had a steep roof similar to the other houses in the neighborhood, but was much larger.

The small gate in the wrought iron fence clanged shut behind them as the two men entered the manicured yard. Passing shuttered windows and petunia-filled window boxes, they came to an office on the right side of the house. The sign on the door read "Robert Schäfer, Architect."

Opening the door, they found a waiting room and a secretary behind a desk. "Herr Schäfer is on the phone. He'll be with you momentarily," the woman said politely in German. A few minutes later the door to the office opened and out walked a stocky blond man in his early 40s, thick glasses perched on his nose.

"Come into my office," he said in fluent Serbian and motioned for them to enter.

Cveja and Walter exchanged surprised glances as they preceded the architect into the room.

"Did I surprise you?" Schäfer said, chuckling behind them. "I was born in Yugoslavia. Novi Sad, to be exact." He gestured toward the chairs. "Please have a seat," he directed. "I'm a Schwabeh [German], a Volksdeutscher, as they used to say. Just before the communists took over, I left the country."

Switching to German, the architect asked Cveja about his education and experience and the types of projects he had worked on. "Yes, I would be interested in hiring you," he said at the end of the interview. "Your professional qualifications and education appear excellent. Your German is good, and I will help you with technical terms so you can work independently."

"When may I start?" Cveja asked. He felt drawn to this man and his firm, despite the fact that the other company offered a better salary and benefits.

"Monday would be fine. Mrs. Schäfer works with me. She is an interior architect." Cveja agreed, the men shook hands, and Cveja and Walter left.

On the way back to Walter's house, both men felt good about the decision. As soon as they entered the house, Cveja phoned Wagner to thank them and decline their offer. That weekend, Cveja spent many hours with Nata, discussing her future and catching up on lost time. Just being in each other's company made them happy.

On Monday, Cveja rose early. He took the trolley bus to the end of the line and then walked 15 minutes to Schäfer's house. He was at the door at 7:45 a.m.

"Come in, come in," Mr. Schäfer said, pleased at Cveja's early arrival. "You're an early bird, I see. Let me show you around the place. As you can see, my office and reception area are here on the ground floor. Upstairs is where my family and I live." He led Cveja outside to the back of the house. "Back here is a garage and an apartment for my in-laws. And the garden house over there," he pointed toward the right side of his property, "contains two drafting rooms. You'll work in the first room, and Herman—he's a draftsman—works in the other room." He checked his watch. "Herman hasn't arrived yet so I'll introduce you later." Schäfer gave Cveja a working drawing scale of 1:50 (2 centimeters = 1 meter) and showed him to the drafting table he would use.

At lunchtime, Cveja retreated outside to the picnic table under one of the oak trees that overlooked the Salzach River. Swollen with rain and the runoff from the mountains, the river sang its special song. Although a mere trickle in comparison, it still reminded him of the Sava and Danube rivers, though the Salzach had a different sound and an unfamiliar smell. Nevertheless, he drank in its scent and the serenity that surrounded him, so relaxed and far removed from his recent desperate plight and the terror of his ordeal. God had truly preserved and led him, and his heart swelled with gratitude. If only Voja were here, he would ask for no more. Yet the reality of their separation left a vacant feeling inside. Despite this beauty and God's abundant blessings, he felt terribly alone.

The first week flew by. On Friday, Mr. Schäfer called him into his office to review the week. "I have examined your drawings. They are precise, and I am very satisfied with your work," the architect said. Needless to say, Cveja went home happy.

With each passing day, the air grew colder. Birch leaves began to turn gold, and flowers wilted and soon disappeared. Cveja enjoyed his job, yet pangs of loneliness and the ache in his heart sliced ever deeper into his being as the days progressed.

One day while Cveja worked at his drafting board in the garden house, Mr. Schäfer came in to visit. Outside the casement window, a young girl about 8 years of age was playing by herself. Cveja had not noticed her before. Mr. Schäfer cranked open the window and called out to the girl. "Susan, why are you not playing with your twin brother?"

At the word "twin," Cveja's ears perked up.

"Papa, Robert hits me," the girl replied, pouting.

"Try again and I will watch you," Mr. Schäfer said. He closed the window and watched her walk over to a young boy who was tossing dry leaves up in the air at the other end of the property.

"Herman told me you had four children, but I didn't know you had twins," Cveja said, a wide grin on his face. "What a coincidence! I have a twin brother, too. We're identical."

Schäfer turned away from the window, a surprised look on his face. "*Unglaublich!* And where is your brother?"

"In Rome. He's waiting for political asylum. As soon as he receives it, he hopes to visit me."

"And what is his profession, if I may ask?"

"Same as mine—he's an architect."

"An architect also! How interesting!" Schäfer grinned. "Does he have a speciality, by any chance?" He seemed to show genuine interest.

"Yes, as a matter of fact, he was the best in our generation for urbanism. He does city planning." Cveja's voice became eager. "Do you think you could employ him too?"

Schäfer raised his eyebrows, his eyes wide. "Why, surely I will have a job for your twin brother!" There was enthusiasm in his voice and an almost excited look on his face, for which Cveja was grateful but which he did not quite understand.

"When he comes to visit, no doubt he will receive a short-term visa, perhaps one month. That is not much time," Schäfer mused aloud. "If anything is to be done, I would need to start things moving in advance. Fortunately the chief of police is my very good friend. I have connections in Vienna as well." His face relaxed, and he smiled. "You know, Cveja, I am very glad to discover this."

As Cveja walked to the trolley bus station on his way home, his spirits soared. Although there was a nip to the autumn air, he felt as warm as spring inside. It was now becoming clear why he had felt drawn to this man. Finding an architect with twins, who had important connections in the government and was willing to help his brother and give him a job, was an incredible break. He felt sure that God was paving the way for Voja. Joy filled his heart and shone out from his face.

The next week a letter arrived from Voja. It said: "Dear Cveja, I've had a routine physical and expect a decision soon. On Wednesday, October 16, I'm going to the Questura di Roma again. If Italy grants me political asylum this time, I'll go straight to the Austrian Embassy to apply for a visitor's visa. If they give it to me, I'll be on the evening train to Salzburg. If Italy rejects me, I don't know what I'll do."

Cveja began praying earnestly.

In the meantime, Mr. Schäfer got busy. "I've been in touch with the chief of police, as well as my contacts in the Labor and Immigration departments in Vienna," he told Cveja one day soon afterward. He cleared his throat, and a frown clouded his face. "I fear there may be a problem, though. My friends tell me that once a person receives political asylum from one country, there is no way another country can grant him asylum too."

Cveja's heart sank. He felt as though he were back at the border again with no hope.

"What my friends suggest is that I try to keep your brother here as a highly qualified specialist," Schäfer continued. "In order to do that I must prove that there is no one in the local job market who qualifies for this position. Starting Monday, I will run an advertisement in the newspaper for two weeks. If no one responds, that will show your brother is not taking a job away from an Austrian citizen. Then I can submit documents to sponsor your brother."

Cveja's spirits revived, and he counted down the days as October 16th neared. The prospect of seeing his brother again flooded him with joy. Yet he dared not expect too much. If Voja did not receive asylum from Italy, he would not be on the evening train. He steeled himself against the possible disappointment even as he arranged for Adolf to drive him to the train station.

On October 16, Cveja arrived at the office early. "Today's the big day!" Mr. Schäfer said, coming into the garden shed to greet him. "If your brother comes tonight, bring him into the office tomorrow with all his documents. I want to meet him. No one has answered my advertisement so far. On Friday it will be two weeks."

All day long every nerve in Cveja's body tingled with anticipation, and his eyes kept darting to the clock. He tried to concentrate on his drawing but saw only his brother's face, his brother's smile.

Later that night after supper, Adolf came by in a borrowed Simca to take Cveja to the railroad station. On the way there only one thought occupied Cveja's mind: Would his brother actually be on the train?

CHAPTER 13

REUNITED AT LAST

Together

The train from Rome was scheduled to arrive at 10:30 p.m. Cveja and Adolf arrived at the station an hour early and waited. Nervous and excited, Cveja paced back and forth along the platform, wringing his fingers and glancing at his watch every few minutes. Adolf waited calmly with him, hands in his pockets.

At last they heard a low hum in the distance. Cveja checked his watch again and grinned at Adolf. It was time. A sharp, shrill whistle slashed the night air. Cveja's face lit up and his eyes brightened. It was the sweetest sound he had heard in a long time. The anticipation made his hands grow sweaty and his heart pound. *Calm down. Relax. Don't set yourself up,* he told himself. *Voja may not be on this train.* He drew a deep breath and exhaled slowly, trying to slow his breathing and heart rate. Soon the locomotive appeared, and the Italian train slid into the Salzburg station and swooshed to a stop. Cveja searched the sea of faces as the passengers disembarked. Some passengers left quickly and alone; others rushed into the waiting arms of friends and burst into gleeful chatter. Frantic to find his brother, Cveja dashed along the platform from one car to the next. Adolf followed, searching for someone who looked like Cveja.

"There he is!" Cveja suddenly shouted, tossing a glance back at Adolf. Voja was descending the steps of a car farther down the line carrying a suitcase in one hand, a rain coat draped over his arm.

"Cveja!" Voja called out when he spotted his brother. His face beamed as he waved his hand. They rushed toward each other, colliding in an embrace and weeping with inexpressible joy. Adolf looked on with tears in his eyes.

Back in the apartment, the world outside forgotten, the two brothers talked, laughed, and wept. Tears flowed over the agonies the other had endured, and tears of uncommon joy were shed because of their reunion.

"It's been five months, one week, and three days," Cveja said. "I hope we'll never be separated like this again."

"So help us God," Voja replied. "The whole time I was in Rome I lived in some sort of fog. Now I feel alive again."

With so much to say and so much time to make up for, the twins stayed up and talked until they could talk no more.

The next morning Cveja arrived at the office late for the first time, and Voja was with him. "My goodness, you really are identical!" Mr. Schäfer exclaimed, a puzzled expression on his face. He donned his spectacles and scrutinized their faces, his eyes darting from one twin to the other. "Aha! I do notice a difference," he said suddenly. "Cveja is a little thinner, and it shows in his face. Otherwise I can't tell you two apart!" He laughed. Since escaping, Cveja had regained a few pounds but was still underweight.

"Now down to business. Let's go into my office," Schäfer said, motioning for them to follow. Closing the door behind them, he gestured toward two chairs. "Please sit down. Voja, did you bring your documents?"

"I certainly did, Herr Architekt. Here they are." Voja handed him his passport and asylum document. Schäfer furrowed his brow and scanned the papers.

"As I expected, a one-month visa." He looked up and nodded. "If you allow me, I will take these papers to the chief of police. We must act quickly." He turned to Cveja. "Why don't you take the day off and spend it with your brother. But first let me show you what you and your brother can work on tomorrow and Monday, just in case I'm not here. This matter may take me to Vienna."

Schäfer put Voja's documents in his attaché case and then accompanied the men to the garden house to discuss the project. He showed Voja the new drafting table purchased for him and wished them a good weekend. Then he left the office. The twins spent a few minutes with Herman, the draftsman, before leaving for the day. Cveja took Voja around the garden and down to the Salzach River before they returned to their apartment.

All that day the brothers talked, sharing more of their experiences while apart. Cveja showed Voja around the church building and the neighborhood and told him of Nata's visit. Mica had not escaped, and she had tearfully returned to Yugoslavia. "Nata was so excited to go to America," he said. "She doubts the authorities will give her a passport again. It was so sad. She was heartbroken when she left. You missed her by just two weeks."

That evening Adolf dropped in. "Pastor Schnötzinger is back from his business trip. He's in his office right now," he said. So the three men made their way downstairs so the pastor could meet the new arrival.

"Duplicates, that's what you are," the pastor observed, laughing, as Cveja introduced his brother.

"I'm the original. He's the carbon copy," Voja quipped.

"Your brother is a joker, too!" The pastor laughed. "One twin is a singer, the other a joker." The group conversed awhile and then went to their separate apartments.

The next morning Cveja left for work, and Voja stayed home. Since it was Friday, Voja set about preparing lunch for Sabbath. They had bought some apples, oranges, potatoes, and cabbage the day before at the weekly farmer's market nearby. A loaf of bread and some leftovers from the pantry rounded out the meal.

"Wait until you see our refugee choir," Cveja told his brother while dressing for church the next morning. "We have a good group, and it's growing. They all live in the refugee camp here in Salzburg."

"Didn't the church have a choir before you came?" Voja asked.

"They still do, and a good one. But they let the refugees participate in the worship service, even though we sing in Serbo-Croatian. They've been wonderfully supportive. Both choirs sing at different times almost every week."

"Interesting," Voja said, pausing to reflect. "Isn't that ironic? The Austrians and Germans were our bitterest enemies in two world wars. Now here we are in their country, enjoying their hospitality and benevolence."

"It's the governments that make the wars, not the people. They've truly welcomed us with open arms," Cveja said. "Good and evil exist on both sides of every border."

On Monday, Voja and Cveja traveled to work together. It was a day for celebration. Mrs. Schäfer came to the garden house to tell them that her husband had indeed gone to Vienna and would not be in.

Two days later when Schäfer returned, he called the twins into his office to report on his trip. "Everything went well," he said, smiling. "I submitted my request to Immigration and the Labor Department. I told them no one responded to my advertisement and that I need Voja to remain as a highly qualified specialist." He tapped his fingers on the desk and raised his eyebrows. "Hopefully, I will get a positive reply—and soon. I asked them to give this matter top priority since our time is short."

The next day before closing, Schäfer called the twins into his office again. "I have been thinking about you two brothers," he said, smiling. "The coincidences in these recent events are startling, don't you think?" He cocked his head to one side. "Do you remember, Cveja, when you first told me you had a brother in Rome?"

"Of course. It was Wednesday, October 2, the day I found out you had twins," Cveja replied quickly.

"Yes, well, what you did not know is that two days earlier I had received advance notice from friends in Vienna that the city of Amstetten intends to expand. Plans are needed for the design of a new planned community which will accommodate 10,000 inhabitants. That's why I asked if your brother had a specialty."

Their curiosity piqued, Cveja and Voja listened intently.

"When you said your brother specialized in city planning, I could not believe it. He was just what I needed for this project!" Schäfer adjusted his glasses and moistened his lips. "It is uncanny, don't you think?" He leaned forward expectantly.

Voja and Cveja exchanged glances. "It certainly seems so," Cveja said, his voice subdued. He thought again of the other job he could have accepted and thanked God for impressing him to take this one instead.

"Yes, indeed!" Schäfer replied. "I do not have definite information yet, but I expect that there will be an open competition for the plans. If and when the notice arrives, I am prepared now." He smiled happily and stood up. "I thought you boys would be interested in this background information."

On the trolley bus that evening the brothers marveled all the way home at the so-called coincidences. "The other job offered more benefits, but it didn't feel right," Cveja told Voja. "Somehow I knew I should take this job instead. Now I know why." He chuckled. "It's amazing how God works. All we need now is a positive response from the Austrian authorities before your visa expires. We have until November 15."

The morning of November 14 dawned cold and gray, the foreboding sky threatening snow. But the twins felt that winter had already moved in—there had been no word from Vienna. Voja had one more day on his visa, and tomorrow he'd have to leave. With the ominous cloud of yet another separation hanging over their heads, the twins left for work as usual. They had no doubt that this was their last day together.

Mr. Schäfer looked glum when they arrived at 8:00 a.m. that morning. "No word yet. I'm sorry," he told them. "But we still have today. Don't give up yet." Two hours later he waltzed into the garden house wearing a grin as wide as his face. *"Gott Sei Dank* [Thank God]!" he exclaimed. "I just received a call from Vienna. My request has been approved." He extended his hand to Voja. "Congratulations, Voja, and welcome! Now you will be able to remain in Austria until you immigrate to America."

It took awhile for the news to sink in, and for a moment the twins sat motionless. Then, bursting with joy, the brothers jumped up to engulf their benefactor in a bear hug. God sat firmly on His throne, and all was right with the world. *But why,* Voja wondered, *do His answers so often come at the last minute?*

Voja's documents arrived in the mail the next week. Cveja immediately took his brother to the refugee office of the World Council of Churches to register. Cveja had registered two months earlier, on September 19, the day after arriving in Salzburg. At that time, he had met the director, a Serb named Boba Zdravkovi (BOH-ba ZDRAV-ko-veech).

"Well, well, well. This must be your brother," Boba said, noticing Cveja enter with a man who looked just like him. The director stopped to greet them, and Cveja introduced the two men.

"I can register you for America," Boba said to Voja. "Fortunately, thanks to President Eisenhower, the quota is still open. Since you are both architects, a profession in demand, you can go on the preferred quota," he said. "A lot of refugees don't qualify and have to wait. America is very choosy, you know. Many refugees go to Canada, Australia, and New Zealand because they don't want to wait. Those countries are looking for new settlers."

"Thank you, but we'll wait. America is where we want to go," Voja replied. Cveja nodded his assent.

While the twins waited, one of the projects Schäfer assigned to them was the renovation of the Altersheim, a home for the elderly, which was located next to the World Council of Churches office building. Erected 40 years earlier, the building needed upgrading to provide more adequate heating and ventilation.

One day while the twins were taking measurements for the new ducts and the dropped ceiling that were to be installed, a disturbance broke out among the elderly residents. Afterward, a very tall, distinguished gentleman approached them "I'm Milivoj Kova evi [MEE-lee-voy ko-VAH-che-veech]," he said in Serbian. "I was a general in the Yugoslav Royal Army. I heard you speaking my mother tongue. What are you young fellows doing?"

After taking a few minutes to explain the project, Cveja asked, "What was that ruckus about earlier? Some of the residents looked very agitated."

"They were terrified," the general replied. "Someone started a rumor that you were installing a gas chamber to gas them."

Stunned and horrified at the thought, the twins were speechless.

"It's over now," the general reassured them. "The administrators discounted the rumor and calmed the residents. You must understand—the Second World War is still fresh in some people's minds." After that the project proceeded to completion without incident.

In the course of working on this project, the twins often dropped by the refugee offices next door to see Boba, and a friendship blossomed between them. When the twins asked him about General Kovačevič, he told them that Tito had sent a personal delegation several times to persuade the general to return to Yugoslavia. Tito had promised the general he'd occupy the same rank and position as before, only this time in the Communist army. "Of course he declined," Boba said. "How could he work for that regime when he believes in freedom?"

One day Boba introduced the twins to two of his associates, Ratko Rančic (RAHT-ko RAHN-cheech) and Duško Pavičevič (DOOSH-ko pah-VEE-che-veech), tall, dark-haired Serbs who had served in the Yugoslav Royal Army with the general. "So why didn't you guys go back?" Voja asked as they ate together.

"We vowed loyalty to our king and to our country. We can't take that back," Ratko said. Boba and Duško agreed. "When Germany invaded Serbia and the Yugoslav army was betrayed and disbanded, a lot of officers escaped.

We fled here. Now this is our life, teaching English and helping our countrymen. If Communism ever capitulates, we'll return to our homeland, but not until then."

Several times the twins invited their new friends over for lunch on the weekend. Always they came dressed immaculately in suits and ties. Usually Voja cooked the meal. Ratko and Duško were bachelors, but Boba had left a wife behind who, as an only child, could not abandon her parents. She had begged him to return but he couldn't. "It was a very difficult decision. And so of necessity we live apart," Boba explained. "It looks like old General Kovacevic's words will come true. 'We'll all return to our homeland one day, but it may be in a casket.'"

One morning shortly after Voja's arrival, Cveja was shaving in front of the mirror when he noticed something odd. "What is this?" he asked out loud. He stopped to take a closer look. There on his chest was a red, swollen spot. "It's itchy," he exclaimed, scratching the spot. "And it hurts."

"Don't scratch, Cveja. Let me see." Voja came over to examine it. "Looks like some sort of nodule." He looked him over. "And there's another one starting on the back of your neck."

Several mornings later Cveja complained, "They're popping out all over me—one on my underarm and another on my hip."

Voja looked concerned. "You'd better see a doctor."

At the doctor's office, Cveja told the doctor who examined him, "They hurt and itch like crazy. And they're getting worse." Voja had accompanied him to the doctor's office and was listening sympathetically.

"H'mmm. These appear to be *furuncles* [boils]," the doctor said, drawing a long face. "Tell me. What has happened to you recently? It must be a woman. Who is the witch?"

"Witch? What do you mean?" Cveja asked, a blank look on his face.

"The woman who's making you miserable," the doctor replied. "It's obvious. This man has a terrible life." He turned to Voja.

"He's not married, Doctor. There is no woman," Voja answered, grinning. "There's just me!"

Both twins chuckled, but the doctor wasn't as amused. "Then you must have suffered some terrible experiences recently—either a lot of stress or a lot of fear. Your blood has been poisoned. It's all coming out in boils."

"I'm a refugee. I spent two months trying to escape from Yugoslavia. I almost got killed a few times," Cveja explained.

"Ah. So that's it—all the adrenalin." The doctor looked closer. "A few of the boils are coming to a head and draining. See, there are some on your back just starting." He finished the examination and took out a prescription pad. "I'll give you something to clear up your condition. The boils may spread more before they get better. Give it time. They'll clear up eventually."

In the weeks that followed, more boils appeared while some of the earlier ones began to dry up. It took many months before the boils vanished entirely. Meanwhile, the twins continued working and waiting, looking forward to a rosy future in a new country. Little did they know that their trials were not yet over.

CHAPTER 14

THE RESCUE

Still clad in his overcoat, Cveja stood in the middle of the apartment, holding his šubara (SHOO-bah-rah, [sheepskin hat]) and the postcard in one hand and unbuttoning his coat with the other hand. He read the scrawled message aloud, "Dear Cveja, please come and rescue us. We're in Wagna Refugee Camp. Come quickly, any way you know how. There are four of us." The postcard was signed Kaca. He set the card on the table, slipped out of his coat, and hung it up. He and Voja had just picked up their mail from the lobby mailbox upon arriving home from work.

"So Kaca finally made it out!" Voja responded. He had discarded his coat and hat and was standing in front of the pantry with his hand on the door, peering inside for something to prepare for supper.

"She must have gotten in touch with Hans, my guide. I sent his name to Djoka in Paris," Cveja said. "The last time I saw her in Novi Sad, she was desperate to escape. Hmmm, I wonder what the problem is." He picked up the card and read it again.

"Where's Wagna?" Voja asked. He opened a can of beans, poured it into a saucepan, and set the pan on the stove to heat.

"Just southeast of Leibnitz. Not far from the Yugoslavian border." Cveja was still standing at the table mulling over the cryptic message.

Voja made a salad and brought it to the table. "She sounds scared. What do you think is wrong, Cveja?"

"Haven't a clue. But I must do something."

Over the meal, their conversation continued. "I know you want to help, Cveja, but what can you do? How can you help them?" Voya inquired.

"I don't know yet." Cveja's brow furrowed. "She said there were four of them. I expected Anica [AH-nee-tsa], her future mother-in-law, and

Pera, her future brother-in-law. Who could be the fourth person?"

Later that evening, Adolf dropped in. Voja was lying on the bed read-ing a newspaper, while Cveja sat at the table writing a letter. Adolf and the twins were good friends now. He was single too, and they enjoyed each other's company.

"Hey, *Zeleni Zamorac* [Green Monkey]!" Voja greeted him. Whenever he visited, the inquisitive, green-eyed pastor scanned the twins' small apart-ment to see if he could spy anything new. Therefore they nicknamed him "Green Monkey," after a curious African species.

Voja sat up, swung his legs over the side of the bed, and laid the paper aside. Adolf took a seat beside him. During the ensuing conversation, Cveja showed Adolf the postcard. It was written in Serbian Cyrillic, which Adolf could read.

"Sounds like some kind of trouble." He returned the card to Cveja.

"Do you know anything about Wagna?" Cveja asked, turning his chair around to face them.

"Not really. Well, yes. I have heard rumors, but who knows if they're true?"

"Rumors? What kind?" Voja asked, leaning toward him.

"Well, they say the guards sometimes sell refugees back to their countries of origin. People from all parts of Yugoslavia are there at the camp, as well as Hungarians who escaped after their revolution."

"That would be enough to scare anybody," Cveja replied, remembering his own fears about being so near the border at Jennersdorf. He stared into space a moment before continuing. "I've noticed that the authorities here treat the clergy with great respect—quite different from an atheistic country. Now, if I were a cleric . . ." He paused. "Adolf, let me see your ID a minute, will you?"

"Sure." Adolf reached into his back pocket, pulled out his wallet, and handed his ministerial intern credentials to Cveja.

"H'mmm. You don't have a picture on it. That's good," Cveja looked up and nodded. "You're a Volksdeutcher, so they'd expect you to have a slight ac-cent," he observed aloud, his eyes on Adolf. "I'd like to borrow this for a day. May I?"

"Sure," Adolf replied. "I trust you. Just don't get me thrown in jail!"

As soon as Adolf left, Cveja went down to the train station to get a schedule. When he got back, he laid out the black suit, white shirt, and black tie which he had purchased after arriving in Salzburg. His favorite color should serve him well on this occasion.

"I'm going to Wagna tomorrow morning," he told his brother. "Explain to Mr. Schäfer that I had to leave. Tell him our friends are in trouble. I'm sure he'll understand."

When Voja got up to go to work the next morning, Cveja had already left. At the end of the day when Voja returned home, Cveja had not yet returned. Voja waited all evening and finally went to bed.

It was 4:00 a.m. when Cveja crept into the apartment, four people trailing behind him. Voja heard their footsteps outside the door and woke up, rubbing his eyes as Cveja flipped on the light. "I waited for you, Cveja, but . . . Kaca, Anica, Pera, you're all here!" he exclaimed after his eyes adjusted to the light. Voja jumped out of bed still half asleep, overjoyed to see their friends and anxious to give them a welcoming hug. Kaca introduced the fourth person as her friend, Lela (LEH-la).

"Oh, Voja, it was terrible," Anica gushed, clasping her hands over her cheeks.

"We lived in constant fear," Kaca said. "Every other day some refugee disappeared. We never knew when one of us might go missing."

"God bless Cveja for saving us," Pera added. "We had no one else to turn to, and we were terrified to stay."

"Well, you're safe here," Voja said, now fully awake. Cveja handed him a robe, and he wrapped himself in it. "I asked Pastor Schnötzinger if you could use one of the rooms on this floor tonight. He gave me the key," Voja continued. "The ladies who live there are out of town now, selling religious books. They won't be back for a couple of months." He shuffled into his slippers, retrieved a key from the counter where he had laid it for easy access, and led them quietly out the door to a room halfway down the hall.

After helping their friends settle in, the twins returned to their apartment and tried to catch a few winks before daybreak. Over breakfast and on their way to work in the morning, Cveja related to Voja the happenings of the previous day.

"I caught the first train yesterday morning. It didn't get to the camp until early afternoon," Cveja explained. "What a difference from Jennersdorf! I couldn't believe it!" He shook his head incredulously. "The camp was surrounded by a chainlink fence topped with barbed wire, and it looked like a prison. The refugees live crammed into old wooden barracks. Jennersdorf was a luxurious mansion in comparison."

"How did you get in?" Voja asked, intrigued. "I've never seen a refugee camp. My escape was easy compared to yours."

"I showed the guard Adolf's ID. The guard assumed it was mine—which was the general idea, of course," he smiled slyly. "I asked to see the camp director. On the way to his office, I spotted Kaca. She was standing near one of the barracks, and she waved at me."

"So what did you do then?"

"I called out to her in Serbian as I walked by. I told her to get her belongings together and everyone who was with her. I said they should wait for me at the gate, and that we had to move fast."

"So what happened then? Did you see the director?"

"He was away. I saw his assistant and showed him Adolf's ID. I told him I had received a postcard from my relatives telling me to come for them." He paused. "Well, they *are* like family, aren't they?" he demanded.

"Of course they are. And what did he say?"

"Well, at first he balked." Cveja mimicked the man's voice. " 'They must be processed,' he insisted. You know what sticklers Germans are for rules. I told him that I had come all the way from Salzburg and must return immediately. I had responsibilities, and the train would be leaving shortly. I promised they'd be safe with me and said I'd take responsibility for their welfare."

"And he agreed?"

"Not immediately. He wasn't sure what to do. He was only the assistant and didn't like making the decision. Finally he handed me a release form which I signed and he approved. When I got to the gate, the four of them were waiting with their bags. The guard let us out with no problem when I showed him the signed release."

"Wow! But you got home so late. What took you so long?"

"The assistant kept us waiting just long enough for us to miss the earlier train. We had to wait four hours for the next one. Thank God, though, it went well. All thanks to Adolf since without his help I could have done nothing."

The next day, Cveja returned Adolf's ID and told him about his experience. Later that day the twins took Kaca, Anica, and Pera to see Boba at the refugee office of the World Council of Churches to register for transit visas to France.

"Kaca's fiancé, Djoka, is waiting in Paris for them with Nikola [NEE-ko-la], the middle brother, and their father," Cveja explained to Boba. "The two brothers defected from a tourist group more than a year ago on the last day of the trip. When they went to Immigration to apply for asylum, they found the office crowded with refugees—six from their own tour group—all claiming to have come to Paris to visit an uncle!"

Boba laughed. "That is truly funny."

"The French offered them asylum a few days later and gave them a permit to work after they passed their physical examinations. Since then they've received their permanent residency."

"Well, people, here are the papers for you to fill out," Boba said, handing each of them a document when Cveja finished the story. "But you will need to get an affidavit of support from your family in Paris to complete the process. Since Anica and Pera are immediate relatives, and Kaca is Djoka's bride-to-be, you can go on a special visa."

While waiting for the affidavit of support to arrive in the mail, Kaca and the others were allowed to stay on in the church building. While living there, they visited often with the twins. Kaca related the story of their border crossing and how her friend came to be with them.

"When I told Lela I was leaving, she begged me to let her come with us. Djoka wrote the name of Cveja's guide in lemon juice in a letter to me. We met him in Slovenia, and he took us to the Austrian border where we had to cross a creek. He wore a leather apron and high boots, and he carried us across one at a time. But when he was carrying me, he stumbled and dropped me, and I got soaked," she said. "It wasn't funny because it was freezing cold and my shoes, coat, and dress actually turned white with ice."

"She got very sick after that," Anica added.

"I sure did, but I didn't know how sick until later," Kaca replied. "Anyway, the guide showed us the white border marker and led us to the road. He told us to follow the road until we got to the railroad station. Then he left. Suddenly we heard a barking dog, and someone shouted 'Halt!' We didn't know who it was and who they saw—us or the guide. We could hear twigs and branches crunching beneath his feet as he made his way back. So we lay down in a ditch beside the road and waited a long time. We were paralyzed with fear.

"Eventually we got up and walked to the railroad station. It was still dark when we got there, and it was closed. So we had to wait outside in the cold until morning. When the stationmaster came, he let us in and started a fire in the wood-burning stove. It felt so good to warm up and dry out." She paused and let out a long sigh before continuing.

"We didn't have enough money for train fare to Salzburg, so we bought tickets to Graz. By the time we arrived there, I was burning up with fever and couldn't go on. So Mama Anica called a policeman, and we tried to explain that we were refugees. Of course, he was German and we couldn't speak the language. But he didn't believe us because we were well dressed, unlike most people who cross the border. So he took us to the police station, and they put us in jail. Can you believe that? Nine days they kept us, questioning us separately again and again. Finally a special police van came and took us to Wagna."

"You've been through quite an ordeal," Cveja said, his voice sympathetic.

"Thank God, you're all right now," Voja added. "You made it in spite of the difficulties."

"Yes," Kaca replied, turning to Cveja. "But if you hadn't given us the name of your guide, we'd still be in Novi Sad. We can't thank you enough for keeping your promise."

"We're supposed to help each other, aren't we?" Cveja replied, then changed the subject. "So how are Djoka and Nikola doing in Paris? They've been there a long time. I bet they've picked up the language by now."

"Probably, but I don't know," Kaca replied. "A nice lady from church who came from Martinique offered them her own bedroom while she slept in the kitchen on an army cot. But they soon ran out of money. Right after they left Yugoslavia, their father sent them a package in care of the Paris Adventist Church. It contained two new pairs of shoes and two jackets. For three weeks they managed to survive on cheap bananas and the few pastries Mama Anica had sent in the box. Then the letter came." She chuckled. "Their father told them that if the dollar bills were too creased, they should press them. This was the first they knew about any money! He had hidden several US$20 bills in the dug-out heels of the shoes and in the shoulder pads of the jackets he sent. Can you imagine? All that time they were wearing money, but didn't know it!"

"I'd love to see them all again," Voja said. "So when is your wedding?"

"Djoka can't get married without me," Kaca laughed, "so whenever I get there and we can make plans. I hope he has enough money saved for a nice wedding and reception in the church."

"I'm sure he will," Pera said. "You've been planning this for a long time."

Kaca nodded and continued, "When their father escaped later, he brought money with him. That same lady helped them find an apartment. She's a French citizen and the one who made an affidavit of support for them so they could stay."

"That's wonderful! We're all indebted to the goodness of strangers, aren't we?" Voja exclaimed. "None of us would have gotten very far without help."

"So how did their father get out of Yugoslavia?" Voja asked.

"The authorities gave him a passport to get some medical treatment in Paris for a war injury. He was a soldier in World War II and had been a prisoner of war, so they were sympathetic. But before they let him out of the country, he had to pay a fine of US$750 because his sons defected. That was big money then. They also told him to bring back his sons. Later, a cousin of his came to Paris determined to bring him back. Somehow they learned of this and laid low for a while. We don't know if the UDBA sent the cousin or if he came on his own."

Since Pera had a nice baritone voice, Cveja immediately signed him up for the refugee choir, and Kaca accompanied the group on the piano. The choir had grown to 26 members now, most of whom were under 30 years of age.

The twins had made arrangements with Mr. Schäfer to work full days Monday through Thursday and only a half day on Fridays, since the sun was setting earlier as winter crept closer. The next Friday they came home early. After lunch, Voja decided to go to a nearby multi-purpose store to buy a loaf of bread. Just as he stepped outside the church building, a *Polizei* car pulled up in front of the entrance. Two policemen climbed out and approached him.

"Guten Morgen. Sprechen sie doch Deutsch [Good morning. Do you speak German]?" one of them asked Voja.

"Ja, Ich spreche [Yes, I speak]," Voja replied that he did. He looked nervously from one policeman to the other, puzzled about what they wanted from him.

The policeman showed him a document written in Serbo-Croatian with a translation in German. Scanning through it, Voja read, "We urgently request the Austrian authorities to help Mrs. Mandi [MAHN-deech] bring back her minor daughter, Lela, who left home without her permission." The document was stamped and signed by the director of the Yugoslav secret police of Novi Sad.

Voja stared at the paper and then at the two policemen.

Just then Kaca stepped out of the building and came up behind him. "What is it, Voja?" she asked innocently. Turning, Voja saw Lela, Anica, and Pera following behind her. Suddenly, the rear door of the police car flew open, and a middle-aged woman jumped out shouting, "Lela, Lela, thank heaven I found you!"

Lela screamed and began trembling. The woman bolted toward the girl, grabbed her, and began tugging her toward the car.

Her minor daughter, Lela. . . . The words on the document stood out in Voja's mind. Both Lela and Kaca were underage, Lela two years younger than Kaca. Whirling around, he whispered to Kaca, "Quick, go back upstairs with Mama Anica and Pera. Go!" They had escaped together, and the police might want to question them. The three immediately backtracked into the building, and the policemen did not try to stop them. Their goal was to locate Lela, who stood crying hysterically and shaking all over.

"I'll give you anything if you come back with me," her mother begged, trying to comfort and hug her at the same time. "Your fiancé is beside himself. You shouldn't have left like that. He's sorry about the misunderstanding and wants you back." Lela continued sobbing, but the shock of the encounter and her shaking gradually began to subside.

During the commotion, Cveja arrived. Kaca and the others had told him of the crisis when they went upstairs. He drew close to Lela and whispered in her ear, "Whatever you do, Lela, don't divulge the name of the guide. Promise me you won't. You mustn't." The Austrian policemen could not understand Serbian and probably assumed that Cveja was trying to convince the girl to go back with her mother.

Lela nodded through her tears. Then her mother grabbed her by the arm and pulled her to the police car where they climbed into the rear seat. The policemen got into the car and moments later, they were gone.

A few days later, a church member offered Kaca and her future in-laws a rental apartment, and the family moved out of the church building. With the money sent by their family in Paris, they could afford to pay for a larger apartment.

Before long, the affidavit of support from France arrived in the mail. Kaca took it to the refugee office of the World Council of Churches. "I'll expedite your documents as quickly as possible," Boba promised Kaca, "but the upcoming holidays may delay the process."

A couple of weeks later, Voja came home from the weekly farmer's market with a large bag of oranges imported from Italy. Produce at the market was less expensive than at the multi-purpose store a couple of blocks away or the small delicatessen across the street, and thus worth the half-mile walk.

When Voja entered the apartment, he found Cveja sitting stiffly at the table, his face as white as chalk. A back issue of the *Politika* newspaper, obtained from Belgrade by one of the refugees and loaned to Cveja, was spread out on the table in front of him. He held one page loosely in his hand.

"Look," Cveja said flatly, pointing to a story as he held out the paper to Voja.

"Two Dead in Murska Sobota," the headline read. The article reported that two secret police agents had gone to the home of a man suspected of illegally taking people across the border. The suspect did not let the agents in but talked to them through the locked wooden door. When the police mentioned the name of a former client, the suspect suddenly unloaded one of his revolvers through the door, killing one of the agents. In the return fire, the other agent killed the suspect inside his house.

Voja shot a questioning glance at Cveja and then continued reading with growing dread.

Slowly Voja put the paper down. "It can't be, can it? Do you think it's possible?" he asked.

Cveja drew in a ragged breath and nodded his head. "I think it is. The details are conspicuously familiar. It sounds like something Hans would do," he said numbly. "Hans lived in fear of being caught. He always kept his loaded revolvers within reach. Somehow, he must have smelled a trap."

"Who could have betrayed him?" Voja wondered.

"I don't know, but whoever it was, the authorities probably beat the information out of him."

"I'm so sorry, Cveja."

"What can I say? Things happen," Cveja replied. His eyes filled with tears. "Hans knew his life was always in danger. That's the risk he took helping people escape. Time and time again, I've asked myself why he didn't escape himself, why he waited." He shook his head slowly. "It doesn't matter now."

For days the newspaper story hung over the twins like a dark cloud. Fear of the UDBA revived, and they wondered if its tentacles could reach them even here in Salzburg. The secret police were known to kidnap refugees off the streets of bordering countries, stuff them into cars, and haul them back across the border. And one evening the twins thought they saw them.

Friends had warned the twins previously of strange figures in long brown leather coats strolling past the church building or lurking in a nearby park. On their way home from work a few days later, Voja and Cveja turned a corner near the church building and stopped in their tracks. Up ahead two strange figures in long, brown leather coats walked along with their hands in their pockets. The twins ducked into a nearby doorway and watched. As the men passed the church, they looked up at the windows. Voja and Cveja waited in the doorway until the strangers disappeared and then hurried home.

Pastor Schnötzinger was still working when they rushed into his office. Breathlessly they told him of the incident and of Lela and the newspaper article.

"We couldn't see the men's faces. And even if we had, we can't say they were actually agents," Voja said. "Brown leather coats are popular."

"It may be a warning. Be very cautious. Let me know if you see any suspicious characters again," the pastor said. "I will report the incident to the police and let the authorities investigate."

After work several days later, Voja and Cveja stopped at the delicatessen across the street from their building to buy some fresh yogurt. As they were leaving, they noticed two men in long, brown leather coats walking toward the store on their side of the street. Backing in quickly, they waited and watched through a window from a safe distance.

The two men strolled slowly past the store, talking and glancing across the street, too far away for the twins to hear what they were saying. This time the twins noticed that they had dark hair and mustaches. After the men disappeared from sight, the twins darted across the street and into Pastor Schnötzinger's office. The light was on, and he was still working at his desk.

Hiding behind the drapes of a window that faced the street, the pastor and the twins looked across the street. The two suspicious strangers had returned and were now standing in front of the delicatessen, each smoking a cigarette. Pastor Schnötzinger immediately picked up the phone and dialed the police.

Within minutes a white and gray police car pulled up in front of the store. Two policemen got out and approached the men. Anxiously the twins and the pastor watched the men take out their wallets and hand the policemen what looked like identification cards. The policemen examined the cards for a moment, then returned them to their owners, gesturing as they did so.

A few minutes later, the men left and the police car drove away. The twins did not find out who they were for certain, but they did wonder if they would encounter them again.

CHAPTER 15

THE UNPARDONABLE SIN

"Our camp is spilling over with refugees. Separated from their families, everyone is edgy and lonely." Viktor (VEEK-tor), a tall man with a dark mustache spoke above the buzz of conversation. "We live in such close quarters that fights often break out and morals deteriorate."

"Not surprising. When you're displaced, you've got nothing to do but wait for your documents to be processed. Living in uncertainty, it's easy to lose hope," one of the other men said.

"Is there anything we can do to help?" another asked.

"They need some distraction. Something to occupy their minds, to give them hope," someone else suggested. "We have our faith, but many of them don't."

"If they had something to read in their own language it might make a difference. If we had some religious literature, that could give them hope," yet another said. "But where can we get some?"

"There is a pastor in New York City, Pastor Kanachky, who prints religious literature in Serbo-Croatian," still another suggested. "If we knew how to contact him, he might send us some brochures that we could distribute."

"Mladen lives in New York. I'll bet he goes to his church. I'll write to him tonight," Voja offered, winding up the conversation.

It was Sabbath afternoon and, as they did every week after church, a group of 20 or more refugees stayed with the twins for lunch. Pastor Schnötzinger had given the brothers permission to use a larger dormitory room for this purpose when it was unoccupied. Today was one of those days, and people were spread out around the room, sitting on beds and folding chairs.

Most of the refugees in this group had come from one of the republics of Yugoslavia—Croatia, Serbia, Montenegro, Macedonia, Bosnia-Hercegovina. A few were of Hungarian or Romanian descent. The twins had known several of the refugees previously in Yugoslavia. Others they had met for the first time in Salzburg. All lived in the local refugee camp in Helbrun, waiting to immigrate to new homes.

Everyone in this group was an Adventist Church member who had, in some way, suffered under communism. They had been fired from their jobs, fined, ridiculed, persecuted, imprisoned, and their children harassed and expelled from school. Many had sacrificed a good part of their savings and risked their lives to escape. Every one of them hoped for a better life, preferably in America. But to be eligible for America, immigrants had to be in excellent health and have a vocation needed in the United States. Other countries, eager to settle their sparsely populated lands, offered incentives and were less demanding.

"*Dragi* Mladen *i* Mela," Voja wrote later that evening after the refugees had gone back to the camp and it was quiet. "Please send us some religious brochures. We want to distribute them to the refugees here in the camp." Voja told them of a few mutual friends who had recently arrived. He put the letter in an envelope and laid it aside to mail in the morning. Then he went to bed.

Nearly three weeks later the twins returned home from work on Friday to find a large package adorned with brightly colored American stamps and customs seals awaiting them in the building's lobby. Voja picked up the package, carried it up the stairs to their apartment, and plunked it on the counter. Throwing his coat over the chair, he tore into the box while Cveja sat down at the table and began sorting through the sheet music he needed for the choir the next day.

"The brochures?" Cveja queried without lifting his head.

"Uh-huh," Voja grunted in reply. He pulled out a small banded packet from the box and slipped out a single brochure. "Well, well, well. What have we here?" he mumbled, scrutinizing the picture on the cover. An attractive young lady with dark hair and eyes sat at a table with an open Bible in front of her. With her elbow resting on the table and a finger on her cheek, she appeared to be in deep thought. Under the picture the title read: "The Unpardonable Sin, What Is It?"

"You American chick, what do *you* know about the unpardonable sin?" Voja quizzed the girl in the picture. Something about her captured his fancy.

"Who are you talking to?" Cveja asked, looking up.

"This girl." Voja showed him the picture. "She's too beautiful to know anything about the unpardonable sin."

"You're talking to a picture?" Cveja said, eyeing the cover. He smiled tolerantly and returned to his sheet music. Voja continued to pull packets out of the box, reading each title aloud as he spread them out on the counter. " 'Why Does God Allow Suffering?' 'Does God Answer Prayer?' 'Where Are the Souls of the Dead?' 'What and Where Is Heaven?' and 'God's Love for Sinners.' "

"Good titles, Cveja. They should make interesting reading. I think these will be good," Voja said, putting the packets back into the box but keeping out one of the brochures. Walking to his night stand, he rummaged through a cluttered drawer for a pair of scissors, and returned to the counter. He cut out the picture, leaving the title of the brochure below it, and then slid the picture into the frame of the mirror that hung over the sink.

"There," he said, stepping back to admire it from a distance. "One day we'll meet, my American friend."

"Oh, you eat cooked prunes," Cveja sputtered after looking up and catching his brother gazing at the picture. "You don't even know who she is." He returned to his task. Below the German words on the sheet music he was writing the Serbo-Croatian translation for the choir members to read.

Voja shrugged and began preparing supper. During supper, as they conversed about the events of their day, Voja snuck occasional glances at the picture of the mysterious girl. Cveja eyed him curiously. "What's gotten into you, Brother?"

"There's a new woman in my life," Voja said with a mischievous grin. "She's playing it cool, but I know she's watching me," he joked.

Cveja coughed patiently and shook his head, eyeing his brother in amusement. Voja had always preferred to play the field while Cveja was the one who usually had a steady date on his arm. Now his brother was flirting with a picture.

When bedtime came, Cveja climbed into bed and pulled the covers over his head. Voja lingered at the mirror. "Good night, Miss America," he whispered, smiling to himself. It occurred to him how ridiculous this was, but somehow he couldn't help himself. A few minutes later he retired for the night.

The next Sabbath after church, the twins' apartment was filled with friends. Since the larger room was not available this day, people sat on every possible horizontal surface, balancing plates on their laps and knees. Some even ate in the hallway.

"The choir sang well this morning," Cveja commented. Then he turned to the mustached man. "You hallelujah'd on time, Fiktor," he said, mimicking the German pronunciation. Viktor and his wife, Ankica (AHN-kee-tsa), new friends from Croatia, had recently arrived and joined the choir. Cveja had begun giving Viktor Bible studies.

"Hey, who's the chick?" Kaca interrupted, suddenly noticing the picture on the mirror.

"Now watch your language!" Voja responded in mock indignation, keeping a straight face. "You're speaking of my girlfriend in America."

"Your what?" Kaca demanded.

"My girlfriend in America," Voja replied.

Kaca burst out laughing. "So what's her name?" she asked, clearly amused. The others quieted down to listen.

"Well, uh . . . actually, I don't know," Voja said sheepishly.

Grinning from ear to ear, Kaca turned to the group. "He doesn't know his girlfriend's name. Can you believe that?"

"Voja, you're losing your touch," someone called out, and the group roared with laughter. Voja the joker was tasting a bit of his own medicine.

"OK, OK. Have your fun." He grimaced and pressed his hand to his chest. "Just know that you've wounded me." Peals of laughter rippled through the room.

"It says there, 'The Unpardonable Sin,' " Kaca observed, pointing to the title.

"That must be her name," someone in the room called out, evoking even more laughter from the group.

"You guys are just jealous," Voja retorted, grinning.

"Where'd you get the picture, anyhow?" Kaca finally asked.

"From Pastor Kanachky. It was on one of his brochures," Voja replied.

"That's Djoka's uncle, you know. Maybe you should find out more about her. After all, she could be married and have a dozen kids. She might even be an old woman by now. You don't know when the picture was taken," Kaca added.

Kaca's comments disturbed Voja, and he made up his mind to find out about the girl in the picture.

"People," Cveja said, swallowing his last morsel of food and depositing his empty plate in the sink. "I'm going downstairs to practice. Come down when you're finished." He walked out the door and down the stairs, his footfalls echoing behind him. Within minutes, stacks of plates and flatware sat piled high in the sink and on the counter. Gradually the group drifted downstairs to the room from which Cveja's "ya-ya-ya-ya-ya-ya-ya" rang out as he warmed up his voice.

After practice, when the rowdy group finally left for the camp, they took with them the box of brochures to read and distribute to fellow Yugoslav refugees. The story of Voja's girlfriend in America, "The Unpardonable Sin," also went with them. Before going to bed that night, Voja penned another letter to Mladen and Mela, inquiring about the girl.

Two weeks later, a reply came in the mail. Voja opened it hurriedly and read it out loud: "Our dear friends, your letter arrived today and I'm rushing to reply. . . . The girl in the picture goes to our church. She plays the organ and piano. She is a lovely Christian, rather serious and reserved. Right now she's not married, but that could change any time. Hurry up and get here. By the way, her name is Ann. We call her Ena (EH-na)."

The news thrilled Voja, though he wondered about the name Ann. Every female name he knew of in other languages ended in a vowel— Marija, Natalja, Mira, Branka. The only other Ann he had ever heard of was Ann Baxter, the American actress. The name Ann sounded strange to him. In any event it was a whole lot better than her new pseudonym. Eyeing the picture of her now, he winked. "You've taken me hostage, my dear Ann," he said. Something tugged at his heart, and he wondered if she even knew he existed.

One evening several weeks later, the brothers returned home from work to find another letter from their friends in New York. When Voja slit the envelope open, out tumbled an out-of-focus snapshot. Squinting, he complained, "Mladen. He's at it again. Even America can't improve his pictures. He's always blamed his camera!" The accompanying letter stated that the family in the picture had just arrived in America. Voja recognized their faces, but there was a girl in the foreground he did not know, and the letter made no mention of her. Voja slid the snapshot into the mirror frame beside the picture of The Unpardonable Sin and forgot about it.

Two days later, Adolf dropped by. Voja and Cveja were sitting at the table, studying English. As usual, he scanned the apartment to see if he could spot anything new. When he caught sight of the snapshot, he walked over to inspect it. He stood there a few moments.

"Aha! I've made a great discovery!" he suddenly exclaimed, turning toward the twins.

"*Zeleni Zamorac,* what is it?" Cveja asked, looking up.

"Didn't I tell you? I'm a genius!" Adolf turned back to the mirror and pointed. "Look, The Unpardonable Sin and the girl in the snapshot are one and the same."

"No, that can't be," Voja protested, jumping up to take a closer look. The snapshot showed a distorted image of a girl who did not look attractive, and he did not want it to be the same person. He joined Adolf at the mirror.

"Oh, but it is! I can prove it," said Adolf. He left the room and returned a minute later with a magnifying glass. Cveja and Voja exchanged amused glances.

Adolf slid the two pictures out of the frame and laid them side by side on the table. Then he bent over to analyze the enlarged images and examine each feature.

"Compare them. See the eyebrows? They have the same arch," he said. "And the eyes? Both girls have dark eyes. Both have dark hair. And the mouth . . ." He straightened up. "I'm telling you, they're the same person. You don't call me 'Green Monkey' for nothing."

"OK, Sherlock. Let me see," Voja said. He grabbed the magnifying glass, bent over, and held it first over one picture, then the other. Straightening up, he retorted, "Come on, Adolf! Where are your eyes? There's no resemblance at all. One is pretty. The other one isn't. One has short hair. The other has long hair." He handed the glass back. "I'm sorry, Adolf, but you're wrong. I'm an architect. I have an eye for these things."

"It's my turn now," Cveja said, taking the glass. He leaned over and examined the pictures for a few moments. "No. They're definitely two different girls," he said authoritatively. He returned the magnifying glass to Adolf. "Definitely not the same, Adolf. Two against one."

"All right, all right, you guys. Stick together. See if I care. But I'm telling you I'm right. Ask your friend in New York. You'll see." Adolf walked toward the door. "And hurry up." The door clicked shut behind him as he left. Before retiring that night, Voja penned another short letter.

Each evening Adolf came by to visit. A couple of weeks later, the brothers came home from work to find another letter from New York. Quickly, Voja read the message from Mela. "Yes, it is the same girl," Voja grumbled, frowning as he read: "The snapshot does not do her justice. You know Mladen's pictures. She's really quite attractive. I think you'll like her."

Letter in hand, Voja went looking for Adolf, but he was not in his apartment. Voja remembered that he often gave Bible studies in the evening.

It was after 11:00 p.m. when Adolf returned, and Cveja and Voja had already gone to bed. He knocked at their door, opened it, and leaned in part way. "Any mail today?" he queried, and then flipped on the light as he entered the room. The twins stirred reluctantly.

"Oh, you eat cooked prunes, Green Monkey! Can't you see we're sleeping?" Cveja complained. He raised his head and squinted at the light, then pulled the covers over his head and rolled over to face the other way.

Voja sat up in bed, and Adolf pulled over a chair. "It hurts me to say so, Adolf, but you were right," Voja confessed. "They are the same girl. The snapshot is not a good likeness."

"I knew it!" Adolf exclaimed, patting Voja on the shoulder as he jumped up. "Sorry to wake you, man. Gotta go now. Good night." He turned off the light and went out the door.

In the days that followed, talking to the girl in the picture became a daily routine for Voja. *Her ears must be burning*, he often thought. As he combed his hair or knotted his tie in front of the mirror, he imagined her watching him. Da Vinci had his Mona Lisa; Voja had his Unpardonable Sin. Eager to meet this person who no longer seemed a stranger, he inquired further. Mela's letters came back, "She's still free, but may not be for long. Please hurry."

CHAPTER 16

A MYSTERY, A CHALLENGE, AND A WEDDING

"Spelling!" the twins exclaimed simultaneously as they exchanged perplexed glances. On the table in front of them the book *English in 100 Lessons*, written in their mother tongue, lay open between them. Each twin had a writing pad in front of him on which he copied down the English words as pronounced in the phonetic Serbian Cyrillic. This evening they had come to Lesson 28, titled "Spelling," a concept they had not encountered before. In other languages they had studied there were rules.

"Maybe when we were 11 we could have learned this language, but not at this age. We're more critical now," Cveja grumbled. As early as the eighth lesson, the peculiarities of the English language had dampened his enthusiasm.

"Let's go on," Voja suggested. He turned back to the book and read the subtitle, "Vowels." Here the European author explained that in English each vowel can have several different sounds. Again they looked at each other with a disgusted frown. In every language they knew, vowels had a single sound except when accent marks altered pronunciation. Each vowel's name indicated its sound: *A* was pronounced AH, *E* was EH, *I* was EE, *O* was OWE, and *U* was OO. So this idea came as a surprise.

"You're right," Voja moaned. "If Tito hadn't considered English a capitalistic language, we could have learned all this in high school. English is very confusing."

"Confusing? More like absurd," Cveja retorted. He got up, shifted his trousers, and paced the floor. "I may be a hairsplitter, but I find no logic in it." Voja remained at the table, doodling *Voja Vitorovi , Vitorovi Voja* as he waited for Cveja to cool down. A little while later Cveja returned to the table, and they resumed their study.

"Double Vowels," Voja read the next subheading out loud. "In English

'OO' is sometimes pronounced 'AW' as in floor or door; but not always. Sometimes 'OO' has the sound of a long 'U' as in stool or fool. Sometimes like a short 'O' as in flood or blood. And sometimes a short 'U' as in book or cook."

"Idiots!" Cveja exclaimed and flung the book to the floor. He got up, opened the door to the balcony, and walked out. It was dark and cold outside, so he came back quickly.

"I can understand exceptions to rules, but English has more exceptions than rules," he said, rubbing his arms as the balcony door banged shut behind him. "French and German have rules, and they're consistent. But English?" He made a sour face. "Even Vuk Karadji [Vook KAR-ah-jeech] wouldn't be able to make sense of this. He did such a good job revising our language that children in first grade learn the alphabet and can immediately read and write. One character for every sound. Here we've got every sound in one character," he complained.

"You're right, Cveja," Voja replied slowly. "But if we're going to America, we have to become Americans and learn the language, like it or not. French won't get you far in New York City." He referred to French because it was Cveja's favorite language.

"This language is just impossible," Cveja griped as they continued studying, and he closed the book.

The next day, when they resumed their English studies after supper, all went reasonably well for a while. "Maybe we're paying too much attention to pronunciation," Voja said. "Remember what Ratko said? The pronunciation shown in textbooks is usually British. Americans pronounce their words differently. So maybe if we just concentrate on learning the words and the meanings, it would be enough for now."

"At least we can try," Cveja said. He leaned back and deftly changed the subject. "Yesterday when we were in Mirabell Park, I heard you speaking Italian to some tourists. It surprised me how fluent you are. Five months in Rome and you practically mastered Italian." He looked back at the book. "We've been studying English on our own for almost a year now, and we're still illiterate."

"Italian is easy, Cveja. It's phonetic, a lot of vowels and open sounds. But English? Well, that's another story." For the next few days they laid the book aside and occupied themselves with other things.

One day toward the end of February, Mr. Schäfer entered the garden shed waving a newspaper and grinning. "Finally it came. It's official now!" he announced. He showed the twins an article in the paper that announced a county-wide competition for plans for the new community in Amstetten. He and the twins had been eagerly awaiting this announcement since it was, after all, the reason Schäfer had sponsored Voja to stay in Austria.

After submitting their request for more information, the application arrived a week later. The form required detailed data concerning the size of the architectural company, names of the staff and their qualifications, a list of previous construction projects, and information about any related experience. Mr. Schäfer and the twins completed the form together, and Schäfer dropped it in the mail.

Several days later a packet came in the mail containing a site plan, topographic map, guidelines for the competition, and specifications for the project. The project required that the plan design include locations for a Roman Catholic church, parish house, elementary school, fire house, single family homes, apartments, and a business plaza to be developed later. Deadline for submissions was set for June 7.

It was early March when the twins began working in earnest on the design. For the next three months they worked feverishly on the plans. On June 3, they walked into Schäfer's office. "Mr. Schäfer, we've completed the plans for Amstetten," they reported happily, handing him the drawings.

"Excellent, excellent!" the architect exclaimed as he reviewed their work. The plans were being submitted under the pseudonym *Die Zwillinge*, meaning "The Twins." He dropped them in the mail and then they waited.

One month later, word of the judge's decision came. Mr. Schäfer practically danced into the garden shed, his face aglow. They had never seen him so delighted. "I have wonderful news!" he said, holding his head high and puffing out his chest. "Our design took first place. We have won the competition! Yes, yes, it's true! And I have a bonus for you." He grinned broadly and handed each of the twins 2,000 schillings. "I can't pay you more than one month's salary," he said, almost apologetically, "since you were on salary the whole time. But I'll gladly give you a month paid vacation."

"That's wonderful!" Voja exclaimed, thrilled at the news. "Now we can go to Paris."

"Kaca and Djoka want us to participate in their wedding," Cveja added. "We'll have to let them know we will be there." Kaca and her in-laws had left Salzburg in March after a farewell party prepared for them by church members. That night the twins wrote a letter to Kaca and Djoka in Paris and began making plans for their trip. The wedding was scheduled for August.

Although the twins were elated that their plans had won first place, receiving the award was even more thrilling for Schäfer. It meant that he would be the chief architect in charge of the entire construction job. He could contract out to anyone of his choosing for each phase of the work. The ongoing project would take years and would earn him a tidy income for perhaps the rest of his life.

In the meantime Voja and Cveja intermittently pursued their English studies. Somehow they made it to Lesson 33. In that chapter the author talked about the more than 4,000 French words incorporated into the English language which were pronounced differently than in French. Aware that they were approaching a slippery slope, Voja proceeded gingerly. "*Nation* is not pronounced nah-see-AWN, as in the French, but NAY-shun. *Station* is not stah-see-AWN, but STAY-shun."

Cveja flung his hands out indignantly. "Where did they find the 'SH' in nah-see-AWN and stah-see-AWN?" he demanded. Reading further he jabbed an accusing finger at the word "colonel." "Look at this!" He read the next sentence. "The word kaw-law-NEL is pronounced KER-nel. KER-nel!" he repeated, fuming. "Where is the *R*?" He snatched up the book and threw it across the room. Luckily Voja turned just as the book flew past him.

"Don't forget that French was the official language of England for almost three hundred years after William of Normandy defeated them in 1066. Things can happen to words in that much time." Voja tried to reason. But Cveja would have none of his excuses. That last chapter had done it; Cveja could not forgive corruption of the French pronunciation. The following night Voja studied the next lesson alone, but his gaze occasionally drifted to his brother, whose head was buried in a book. At Cveja's request, their sister Vera had sent them certain books in Serbian, and he was rereading *The Captain's Daughter* by Pushkin.

As summer progressed and the weather warmed up, their refugee friends began to leave for their new home countries. Several months before, Adolf had left for the Adventist college in Collonges-sous-Salève. Since then, he had met a girl there, and they had fallen in love. They planned to marry and had already signed up for mission service in Cameroon. Viktor and Ankica and several others in the group departed for Canada. Others immigrated to Australia after their papers were processed. Wherever the refugees went, the tale went with them of Voja's girlfriend in America named The Unpardonable Sin.

By the end of the summer all their refugee friends had gone. The Yugoslavian choir was silent now, and on Sabbaths the twins returned from church to an empty apartment. Since the Yugoslavian immigration quota to the United States had been filled for the year, the twins decided to wait there in Salzburg until it reopened again the following year.

In August, Voja and Cveja took the train to Paris for Djoka and Kaca's wedding and a long-awaited visit with their friends. There, in the city of lights, they toured its many famous sights—the Arch of Triumph, the Eiffel Tower, Notre Dame Cathedral. One of the bedrooms in the Bikicki's (Bee-KEE-tsky's) apartment had been converted into a dormitory room. A wall of boxes piled high to the ceiling provided a divider and some sense of privacy. On one side slept the three Bikicki brothers; on the other side, the twins.

On August 8, Kaca and Djoka tied the marital knot in a lovely ceremony performed by a French pastor in the Paris Seventh-day Adventist Church. Kaca and the Bikicki brothers had picked up quite a bit of French during their stay and were conversant in the language. Cveja served as *kum*, best man, while Voja joined Nikola and Pera as an usher. The family had made many friends, and after the ceremony about 200 church members, family, and friends retired to the social hall in the basement of the church for a sumptuous feast prepared by the ladies.

The following Tuesday, the newlyweds prepared to leave for their honeymoon. Since Djoka's parents were not permanent residents, they could not work, but their gainfully employed sons had pooled their resources to purchase a family car, a Chevy Fregata. And so, following plans made before the wedding, the newlyweds, the in-laws, and the twins set out for a joint honeymoon/family vacation. With four people jammed into the front seat of the car and four in the back, the roof rack strapped with luggage, and the trunk filled with camping and cooking equipment, they left Paris and ventured into the French countryside. A young French couple from the church accompanied them in their own vehicle part of the way. Except for the newlyweds, who did not complain, no one at the time thought much of the unusual arrangement for the couple's honeymoon.

During the month of August, offices and factories throughout France close for vacation, so the roads were flooded with traffic and the tourist sights with visitors. In Avignon, the group viewed the massive, gothic Palace of the Popes, used as a papal residence during most of the 14th century, and later by two anti-popes during the Papal Schism. As they traveled south, they pitched two tents at night. The groom's parents slept in one tent and the rest, six in all, slept in the other. The poor newlyweds had hardly any time to be alone.

When they reached the Adventist college in Collonges-sous-Salève, they spent the night, and the next day crossed the border by bus into Geneva, Switzerland, for a one-day tour. With only temporary documents, the groom's parents could not cross the border and remained behind with the family car.

After traversing the narrow winding roads across the French Alps, they finally came to the seaport city of Marseille. Dominating the skyline atop a limestone outcrop, the basilica of Notre-Dame de la Garde, with its gigantic gilded statue of the virgin and Child, overlooked the deep blue waters of the Mediterranean Sea. Numerous yachts and fishing boats navigated the harbor or docked in the port. After spending a few days touring Marseille, they started slowly back.

At the end of their month-long vacation, the twins returned to Salzburg. A letter from the World Council of Churches awaited them. A physical examination had been scheduled for Cveja prior to being issued an entry visa for America. Because of the frequent incidence of tuberculosis, all applicants were thoroughly screened. Even the slightest indication of contact with tuberculosis resulted in immediate disqualification. "Finally we're making some progress," Cveja rejoiced.

In early October Cveja received his American entrance visa. Thrilled to have completed the process, he was now cleared and ready to go to the United States. The visa, dated October 4, 1958, and valid for four months, would expire on February 4, 1959. He could enter America any time up until that date. If, for any reason, he did not enter within that time, the visa would expire and could not be extended or renewed.

Voja, meanwhile, had received nothing—not a word about a physical exam or his papers. "Maybe my papers have been held up in Italy," Voja rationalized. Unbeknownst to him, though, foul play was afoot.

CHAPTER 17

ACCUSED

"Guten morgen." The attractive receptionist at the American Consulate slid open the window of the glass enclosure. "How may I help you?" Much to Voja's relief she greeted him in German. He still did not feel comfortable enough with his knowledge of English to attempt to speak it.

"I have a 10:00 o'clock appointment with the General Consul, Herr Michelin," he said. He pushed toward her the letter he had received in the mail. "My name is Vojislav Vitorovic."

"One moment," she said, scanning the letter as she picked up the phone. As she spoke into the receiver, Voja turned around to survey the lobby. A Persian-style rug skirted by 10 upholstered French provincial chairs delineated the pleasant waiting area. A few pieces of furniture, lamps, and plants added to the decor, and an arrangement of freshly cut flowers on the table added a clean, sweet scent to the air.

"The consul is expecting you upstairs," he heard the receptionist say, and he turned back to face her. She pointed him to the staircase in the rear.

As Voja walked across the lobby, his heels clacked on the polished parquet floor. The lobby was empty, and each sound echoed in the high-ceilinged room. As he climbed the wooden staircase, his mind bristled with questions. *What was holding up his papers? Why had the American consul summoned him? Could there be some problem?*

All of Cveja's contacts had been through the mail. Cveja had completed his week-long physical examination and received his entry visa for America more than a month ago. Voja had received no word at all. Until recently, the rationalization that his papers were stalled in Rome had assuaged his anxiety—it had taken five months for Italy to offer Voja political asylum, but

Cveja had received his from Austria within a week. Now he felt a strange foreboding that something was terribly wrong.

At the top of the stairs he entered an unfurnished foyer in which three of the walls each contained a paneled oak door. A sparkling crystal and gold chandelier hung from a circular plaster medallion in the ceiling. Waiting expectantly, Voja kneaded his fingers and bit his lip, wondering which of the doors would open.

Before long the door on the right opened toward him, and two men in dark suits and ties walked out into the foyer. A tall, younger man wearing thick glasses came out first, and a middle-aged gentleman, his brown hair graying at the temples, followed. The younger man beckoned to Voja and went back into the room. Voja followed, and the middle-aged gentleman walked behind him.

Passing through the doorway, Voja brushed against the leather-tufted padding on the inside of the door and caught a whiff of the musky leather. A second door, also leather padded, abutted the first and opened into the room. *Two padded doors—the sign of a soundproof room*, Voja noticed, and his anxiety increased.

Inside the room the younger man gestured for Voja to sit at a large oak table surrounded by padded leather chairs. On the far wall a heavily draped window limited the amount of light that entered. The two men took seats across the table from him.

Voja sat rigid on the edge of his seat, his hands fidgeting in his lap. He looked from one somber face to the other, waiting for one of the men to speak. In return, four scrutinizing eyes fixed their gaze on him. The younger, bespectacled man began. Speaking in German, he introduced the older man as the American consul, Mr. Michelin. For the first time, Voja noticed the consul's dark penetrating eyes.

"Drhmehrrywhrrldeawhyrrryyydheer?" the American consul began speaking. This was the first time Voja had heard spoken English. The words seemed to run together in one garbled sound, and he could not distinguish separate words. The man sounded as though he had a hot potato in his mouth as he talked.

The younger man, the interpreter, began translating the consul's words into German. "Do you have any idea why you are here?" Voja's eyes shifted from the consul to the interpreter.

"No, sir, I don't," he replied in German, shaking his head. The interpreter translated his answer into English for the consul.

The consul spoke, and again Voja heard only indistinguishable sounds. The interpreter translated the consul's words. "I'll come right to the point," he said. "We've called you here to give you bad news. Someone has accused you of being a Communist spy."

The words struck Voja quick and hard. For a long, shocked moment, he sat stunned and senseless. He felt like a boxer caught off guard by a powerful blow to the gut. Slumping back in his chair, he gripped the leather arms. His mind reeled, and his world went dark.

The consul was speaking again, and the interpreter translated. "In cases such as this," he was saying, "we automatically close the person's file. His chance of emigrating to the United States is zero."

His heart pounding, Voja struggled to make sense of what was happening.

"However, your case puzzles me," the consul continued. The consul leafed through a file that lay open on the table in front of him, obviously Voja's. He picked up one of the papers. "I see here that you have an identical twin brother named Svetozar who has already received his visa."

The consul paused for a moment. "You both have the same father, the same mother, the same religion, the same profession." He counted off the similar items on his fingers and then threw his hands up. "Yet one of you is a good boy, and one is bad." He leaned toward Voja, who got the emphasis, even in English. "We have no way to verify or disprove such an accusation. Asking the Yugoslav authorities, of course, would be pointless. So we usually just close the accused's file." He sat back in his chair.

The voices of the two men sounded hazy and distant. Their words alternately pounded Voja, first in English, then in German. It was over. His hopes melted away.

"However," the consul leaned forward again and put his elbows on the table, his hands clasped under his chin. "I've decided to make an exception this time and give you a chance." Voja's head began to clear, and his eyes widened as the interpreter translated the consul's words into German.

The consul continued. "Can you provide me with a letter from your church? Someone in Yugoslavia who could verify that you're a regular member in good standing, and not a Communist?"

"Yes, I can do that," Voja heard himself say too quickly.

"Good! Time is of the essence. As soon as you get it, bring it here. You must proceed quickly," the consul concluded. He and the interpreter rose from their chairs and nodded. The meeting was over, and the interpreter ushered Voja out into the foyer.

In a daze Voja descended the stairs, walked through the lobby, passed the receptionist without a word, and went out the door. Questions swirled through his mind. *He, a Communist spy? Who could have accused him? Why would anyone do such a thing?* He had promised the consul that he'd get a letter from Yugoslavia verifying his church membership. How could he do that? The authorities censored mail in and out of the country and his letter might never be delivered.

Suddenly, as if awakening from a dream, his situation became all too clear. There was no way to prove his innocence, and after all the struggles he and Cveja had endured, his brother would go to America without him.

With a heavy heart he boarded the trolley bus to his stop and then walked the remaining half mile to the apartment. The lively chatter of people who streamed in and out of the quaint shops and boutiques along the way seemed to mock his despair. Even the sweet fragrance wafting into the street from the *pâtisseries* was unappreciated. Oblivious to the traffic and the people bustling about, Voja was besieged with gloomy thoughts.

While waiting in Rome for asylum, Voja had heard the story of a young Serb who had escaped to Trieste and applied to go to America. His father was an American citizen. But some unknown person had accused the Serb of being a spy. The last Voja had heard, 10 years had elapsed and the man was still waiting in Trieste—by now a permanent resident. As far as he knew, the man never did make it to America.

Voja thought of his recent separation from Cveja. Five months, one week, and three days of torment for both of them—torment not just because of their trying circumstances, but because of their powerful need to be together. How could they possibly endure another extended, potentially indefinite separation?

Dark rain clouds descended in the sky, and a freezing drizzle began to fall. When he reached the building that had been their home for more than a year, his *šubara* was soaked, his face tingled from the cold, and he was shivering.

"You look dreadful," Cveja remarked when he saw not only his brother's drenched clothes but the despondent expression on his face also. Voja knew Cveja had been praying. It was their daily practice and continuing source of strength. After drying off and changing his clothes, Voja poured out his tale of woe. "I'll never see America, Cveja. You'll have to go without me."

"No way, my brother. America would mean nothing if you weren't there. We could settle here in Austria. We have a job, and Mr. Schäfer is willing to sponsor us as permanent residents. Or, even better, we could go to France. Kaca and Djoka are there. Then we can speak *la langue Français*." He forced a smile. "We won't ever be separated again."

A knock at the door interrupted their conversation. Pastor Schnötzinger stood there, smiling. "Well, how did it go?" he asked, entering the room. Voja had informed him of the appointment at the consulate.

"Pastor, I'm in big trouble," Voja lamented as the pastor joined them at the table. "Someone accused me of being a Communist. Not just a Communist, but a spy. I can't imagine who or why."

The pastor frowned. "That can't be. How is that possible?" he protested.

"That's what I thought, too. But it happened. The consul said that in these cases, he normally closes the file since he can't investigate. But for some reason, he offered me a chance. He asked me if I could get a letter from Yugoslavia. Something to say I'm not a Communist, that I've been a Seventh-day Adventist member in good standing for years." His forehead wrinkled, creasing his brow. "I don't know why I said I could. The trouble is, the mail is unreliable, and the authorities censor it both ways."

The pastor thought for a moment. Then his eyes brightened, and a broad grin spread across his face. Jumping up, he threw open his arms and peered over his spectacles. *"Keine Sorgen, mein lieber bruder Vitorovi* [Not to worry, my dear brother Vitorovi]!" he bellowed. "Tomorrow I go to Switzerland. The church's Southern European Division is having its annual meeting. Pastor Lorencin from Yugoslavia should be there. Surely he can provide the letter for you." He gestured enthusiastically with his hands. "Write him tonight. I'll take your letter with me tomorrow morning. When I come back, I'll bring you his reply. Neither letter will see the mail or the censors!"

Astonished, the twins stared first at the pastor and then at each other. The news was incredible, the timing of the pastor's trip perfect. Perhaps there was still hope. Before retiring for the night, Voja wrote a letter to Pastor Lorencin.

That night as they lay awake in bed, the twins recalled the promise, "Before they call I will answer; while they are still speaking I will hear" (Isaiah 65:24, NIV). Even before they knew the problem existed, God had prepared a solution. "Forgive me for my lack of faith," Voja prayed. Praising God, he drifted into a pleasant sleep.

The next day, while Cveja and Voja were at work, Pastor Schnötzinger boarded the train for Bern, Switzerland. Among the papers in his leather briefcase, he carried Voja's letter. Four days later he returned late at night. Early the following morning before the twins left for work, he visited them in their apartment.

"Mission accomplished!" he announced brightly. He stood in the doorway beaming and handed Voja an envelope.

Voja hastily opened the envelope and pulled out three legal-sized sheets of yellow ruled paper on which Pastor Lorencin had handwritten a letter to the American consul. Voja read it out loud while Cveja looked over his shoulder.

"Honorable Sir, as President of the Yugoslav Union of the Seventh-day Adventist Church for the past twenty years, I wish to testify that I am personally acquainted with Vojislav Vitorovic and his entire family. He and his twin brother, Svetozar, his mother, and three sisters are all church members in good standing. I can personally attest to the fact that he is not now, nor has he ever been, a Communist. . . ."

Pastor Lorencin went on to list several reasons why he believed this to be true, including the fact that he had known the twins since they were 11 years of age, that their family had suffered under communism and lost their businesses, and that both brothers held positions of trust in the church and were active participants. Next to his signature, the letter bore the stamp of the Southern European Division of Seventh-day Adventists.

"Wonderful!" Voja shouted excitedly. "Pastor Schnötzinger, you're an angel in disguise!" He wrapped the pastor in a jubilant hug.

"A corpulent angel, perhaps," the stocky pastor said with a grin.

"If this letter doesn't help, nothing will. I'll take it to the consulate right now." Voja turned to Cveja and said, "Tell Mr. Schäfer that I'll be late."

"Don't worry, and good luck!" Cveja said cheerfully.

When Voja arrived at the American Consulate, he was ushered again into the same soundproof room and seated at the same oak table where his hopes had been decimated. The American consul and German translator sat again across from him as they had before. Enthusiastically, Voja handed the consul his letter.

The consul took the letter in hand and scanned the pages, a look of surprise on his face. "Hbergghnnlllkhwwhrrrjlk." Again Voja heard the garbled sounds he could not decipher. "How did you get this so fast?" the interpreter translated into German. The letter was written in Serbian Cyrillic, and the consul, a typical American, obviously knew only English. As the consul leafed through the letter, Voja told him about Pastor Schnötzinger's trip and the meeting in Bern, Switzerland. The consul handed the letter back.

"This letter will have to be translated into German, and from German into English. Both translations notarized. You need to find a certified translator," the interpreter relayed the consul's instructions. "Try to get this back to us today," he urged.

Returning to the church building, Voja burst into the pastor's office, breathless and cold. A frigid wind was blowing outside, and a light snow had begun to fall. He took off his gloves and rubbed his hands together. "Pastor Schnötzinger, I need your help again."

After hearing his tale, the pastor phoned a Serbian acquaintance of his who had an office nearby with qualified translators who could do both translations.

By this time, it was almost noon. Voja hurried over the wet streets past the Mozarteum to the man's office a few blocks away. The light snow that had been falling earlier had stopped. Only the dirt squares around the trees along the street retained a thin blanket of white.

"Pastor Schnötzinger called about this letter," he told the man in the office after introducing himself. He handed him the letter.

"Our Serbian translator is on his way here from our other office," the man said. "He should be here any minute. We'll have these for you in about three hours."

"I'll wait," Voja told him.

Voja's watch showed 3:30 p.m. when the translator finished. He handed Voja the original letter as well as the two typed letters, each signed and bearing the translator's notary seal. Voja thanked him, paid the fifty schillings, and left.

By the time he arrived at the American Consulate, it was 4:30 p.m., nearly closing time. To his relief the consul was still there. Back in the second floor office, the three men sat around the oak table once more.

"The English translation and the original handwritten letter will go to Washington, D.C.," the consul said through the interpreter. "My own remarks and recommendations will be included. I will keep the German translation in your file here." He paused. "This correspondence will go through diplomatic channels. Regular mail is too slow. But I must warn you, even through diplomatic channels, the process usually takes six months." He fixed his penetrating eyes on Voja.

Voja's heart sank. "But . . ." He started to speak and then stopped. He didn't have that kind of time, and the consul knew that. But the situation was out of his hands.

"Washington will make the final decision," the consul concluded.

It was November 14 now. Cveja's visa would expire on February 4. Washington's decision could go either way, and he had less than three months to receive an answer.

CHAPTER 18

THE DEADLINE APPROACHES

"Nothing!" Voja complained, peering into the empty mailbox. It was the first week of December 1958, and they had just returned from work. Since his meeting at the American Consulate, the long awaited reply from Washington dominated his waking thoughts. Would his application be approved? And would the answer come in time?

"A month has passed since my meeting," Voja said as he and his brother relaxed after supper. They had turned on the radio, and Beethoven's Ninth Symphony played in the background. Earlier their conversation had excluded the subject but now it surfaced. "I know it's a long shot, but . . ."

"We still have until February 4. My visa's good until then," Cveja interrupted.

"That's less than two months," Voja responded. He turned to the calendar on the wall and stared at the numbers. "Pan American's refugee flights fly twice a month. We need to get word from the consul in time to get a seat on one of those flights."

The December days quickly grew colder and wetter. Sullen skies daily produced either cold rain, snow, or sleety showers. Snow soon accumulated in speckled white carpets within Salzburg's beautiful gardens and parks and piled in dirty mounds along the busy streets. Remarkably, the city streets and sidewalks were kept relatively clear.

Even the normally fast-moving Salzach River curving through the center of Salzburg froze over for miles, allowing children to play on its slick, solid surface. Skiers of all ages swarmed everywhere—in the narrow traffic-free streets of the old section, in plazas and parks, and even on roads where drivers proceeded cautiously. Atop Monchsberg ridge, Hohensalzburg, Central Europe's largest preserved fortress, was adorned with frozen white clumps of snow clinging tenaciously to its mighty walls and towers. Icicles, like crystal jewels, hung suspended from the Gothic roofs.

Each day upon returning from work, the twins checked the mail. But each day there was no word from the consulate. Voja found his mood alternating between optimism and despair. One minute, he pictured himself sitting in Mladen's home in New York City wearing jeans and a cowboy hat, drinking 7-Up, and watching TV. The next minute, he saw himself at the airport in Munich waving goodbye to the plane that would carry Cveja to America without him. And what about his Unpardonable Sin? Would he ever meet her? Did she even know he existed? Would she wait? In spite of the uncertainty, the twins prayed for guidance and the willingness to accept whatever outcome God would allow.

As Christmas drew near colorful lights went up along the downtown streets, fragrant green garlands adorned the lampposts, and last-minute shoppers crowded the sidewalks. Still the American Consulate remained silent.

On Christmas Day a Bible worker who lived in an apartment upstairs invited the twins for Christmas dinner. *"Fröhliche Weihnachten* [Merry Christmas]!" the man and his wife greeted them when they arrived. In this home the twins saw their first manger scene, a western symbol for Christmas. The beautiful ceramic figures of Mary, Joseph, and baby Jesus graced the credenza in the small dining room. During the evening, each pair shared their traditions.

"The Serbian Orthodox greeting is, *'Hristos se rodi!'"* the twins explained. "The response is, *'Vaistinu se rodi!'* Translated, that means, 'Christ is born!' and 'Indeed, He is born!' I like the sacredness of that salute," Voja said.

"The most fun for us when we were kids was on Christmas Eve when the yule log was brought in," Cveja continued. "Parents hide oranges, figs, nuts, and special treasures in a blanket of straw under the dining table for the children to ferret through."

"But it's not figs and nuts I need now. It's an American visa," Voja said sadly.

The couple nodded their understanding.

As the year 1959 approached, and the expiration date of Cveja's visa drew ever nearer, the twins' anxiety grew. Mr. Schäfer had received a big project, and they didn't want to start it only to leave part way through. Excavation for the new community of Amstetten had not yet been officially approved. So at the end of December the twins resigned from their job. They could live on their savings while trying to decide their future. With mixed feelings, they bid farewell to the architect and his family, of whom they had grown very fond.

"Are you sure you won't stay? You know I would sponsor you. You could remain here," Mr. Schäfer again offered. But the twins' thoughts had turned to the possibility of living in France. Austria's winters were long and cold, and they did not like the frigid weather. Besides, they wanted to put more distance between them and the Yugoslav border, just to be safe.

The second week of January arrived. Voja sat in the apartment staring at the calendar. Only five weeks remained until Cveja's visa expired. Cveja lay on the bed reading a borrowed copy of *Anna Karenina* for the umpteenth time.

"Cveja," Voja interrupted. "We've got to talk."

Cveja looked up, noting the somber tone in Voja's voice. He laid aside his book, swung his legs over the side of the bed, and sat up.

"I can't let you sacrifice yourself. This is your one chance to go to America. You can't let your visa expire. Later, once you got settled, maybe then you could sponsor me."

"I'd have to be an American citizen to do that. It would take years," Cveja replied. "No, brother, my decision is final. I'm not going unless you go with me, not even to America." His voice sounded firm. "Whatever happens, we'll stay together." He adjusted his pillow, lay back down again, picked up his book, and resumed reading.

Another evening Cveja suggested, "Why don't we go to the French Consulate?" Their recent conversation had made him start thinking. The second week of January had come to a close with no word from the American Consul. "We've talked about the possibility of living in France. Why don't we inquire and see what they tell us."

A two-hour electric train ride the next Monday morning took them to the French Consulate in Innsbruck, the Tyrolean capital surrounded by spectacular mountains. "So you're both architects?" the French consul asked after they stated their request. "We can use architects in France." After some discussion he took their passports and left the room. When he returned several minutes later, he handed them back with a flourish. *"Voilà!"* he declared. "I've given you entry visas valid for ten years. During that time, you may enter and leave France at any time. You can live there and work. If you decide to make it permanent, you can take the necessary steps." Overjoyed, the brothers thanked the man and left.

The twins both spoke French, so language presented no problem, although Cveja's pronunciation was much better. With Plan B now in place, they returned to Salzburg happy and prepared to await the outcome of Voja's application for America. If America rejected him, or if the answer did not come in time, they would settle in France. Cveja would be relieved not to have to bother with English. They would not get to see New York's Empire State Building or Fifth Avenue, but Paris had the Eiffel Tower and the Champs-Élysées. Not a bad exchange. Life was simple enough when one accepted what it offered. Most of all, though, Voja would regret not meeting his Unpardonable Sin.

A few days later, on January 23, they arrived home from the market to find a letter in their mailbox. Voja pulled it out eagerly. "It's from the American Consulate!" he shouted. The letter had finally come. "This may be the decision," Voja said, hesitating a moment before slitting it open. Then he pulled the letter out of the envelope.

It was brief, and Voja read it quickly. "Dear Mr. Vitorovic, Please come to the American Consulate office on Tuesday, January 27, at 9:00 a.m. Bring all your documents with you. We request that your brother, Svetozar Vitorovic, accompany you and bring all his documents as well." It was signed, "Andrew Michelin, Consul General, American Consulate."

Voja looked up, suddenly feeling gloomy. "This is it," he said, holding out the letter to Cveja. "They want you to come, too—probably to take away your visa."

Cveja reread the letter slowly, then handed it back. "Well, at least we'll find out where we stand," he responded with a resigned sigh.

CHAPTER 19

AN ASTOUNDING TURN OF EVENTS

The next Sunday Ratko and Duško, their friends from the refugee office of the World Council of Churches, came for lunch.

"Boba sends his apologies. Something came up at the last minute," Ratko explained as the two men entered the apartment. He sniffed the air. "M-m-m. Is that *podvarak* I smell?" He breathed in the savory aroma. Voja had prepared the cabbage dish with smoked beef just the way the men liked it.

"I must be in heaven," Duško announced. He loosened his tie and flipped it over his shoulder as they sat down at the table. The twins had brought in two more chairs from another room.

After lunch the four men relaxed and talked. "Somebody accused me of being a Communist spy," Voja told the two men for the first time. And then he related how Pastor Schnötzinger had gone to Switzerland and brought back a letter from the church which Voja submitted to the American Consulate. "A couple of days ago a letter came from the Consulate. They want me to come in on Tuesday, along with Cveja. He's to bring all his papers. I'm worried they'll revoke Cveja's visa."

"Not necessarily," Ratko said. "It's never over until it's over, you know." He cast a knowing glance at Duško, who gave him no indication that he shouldn't speak. Ratko continued. "I probably shouldn't tell you this, but your case would never have been reconsidered if . . . if it hadn't been for Boba."

"Boba? What do you mean? What does he have to do with this?" the twins asked simultaneously.

"A couple of months ago, probably right after you saw the consul, Duško, Boba, and I were sitting together in a cafeteria drinking coffee one Sunday when Michelin came in and came to our table. He pulled Boba aside to talk to him privately," Ratko explained.

"About Voja?" Cveja asked.

"Yes. Michelin wanted to know how well Boba knew you fellows. He said there was a serious problem with Voja's application. He would have to close the file, but for some reason he was reluctant to do so."

The twins sat open-mouthed in rapt attention, leaning in close to listen. Ratko continued. "Boba told how he came to know you while you worked on the *Altersheim*. He thinks very highly of you both. All kinds of people come through our offices, and he took a special liking to you." Ratko paused and smiled. "You're not supposed to know this," he repeated, glancing again at Duško. "Boba told Michelin that he trusted you implicitly. Then he did something dramatic. He extended his hands and said, 'I'd put these hands in the fire for this man. I'm convinced he's innocent. He could not be a Communist.' "

The twins sat silently, stunned by the story and humbled by Boba's confidence in them.

"We never realized how much our friendship meant to him," Voja said. "We certainly think a lot of him."

"Did Boba tell you this himself?" Cveja asked, his voice rising.

"No," Ratko shook his head. "He'd never do that! It was Michelin who told me—in strictest confidence. Now I've told you, and now you know. But you must never let on that you know!" he said emphatically. "Boba would be terribly embarrassed and upset with me."

After their friends left, the twins, still awestruck, reflected on the conversation. "Maybe there is still hope," Voja said. "As Ratko said, it's never over until it's over."

"Just like a novel," Cveja mused. "Tuesday we go to the next chapter."

Encouraged by the visit the twins felt more hopeful about their upcoming meeting at the consulate. A few days yet remained. Finally, January 27 arrived, the day on which their future would be decided.

Cveja and Voja awoke early. Neither had slept well, and they managed to choke down only half of their breakfast that morning. In identical blue suits and ties, they stepped out of the building into yet another dull morning.

"Gray again. Every day is gray," Voja complained. "Gray winter skies, gray circumstances, gray future. Life seems to exist in the gray zone."

"Well at least it's not snowing," Cveja replied. "We're in transition."

An early morning motorcyclist roared past them as they walked to the trolley bus that would take them to the classical-looking building of the American Consulate at 13 Giselle Strasse. Inside the lobby, they stopped at the glass partition. The same efficient, attractive receptionist looked up and greeted them, directing them upstairs.

They plodded up the steps and waited in the upstairs foyer, fidgeting and staring at the doors. Voja did not have to wonder which door would open. He knew. And he watched it closely for the two men to emerge.

Before long the door on the right opened, and the American consul appeared. This time he walked out alone. Puzzled, Voja peered through the doorway expecting the German translator to emerge, but he was nowhere to be seen. *Now that's peculiar*, he thought. *How will we communicate with this American? English is obviously the only language he speaks.*

The consul walked up to the brothers, put his hands on his hips, and smiled for the first time. This was definitely not his official consul face or his usual aloof manner. Then the man opened his mouth and spoke in perfect Serbian, *"Ko ce da časti* [Who is treating]?" The corners of his mouth began to twitch and then a hearty laugh erupted.

Shocked, Voja and Cveja drew back, their mouths hanging open. Cveja flung a why-didn't-you-tell-me look at Voja, but that glance told him that his brother was no less surprised.

"Aha! I got you, didn't I?" the consul continued in Serbian, looking greatly amused at their astonishment. Then he led them through the padded doors into the soundproof room where they sat around the all-too-familiar table.

"Nobody, and I mean nobody, knows I speak Serbian," the consul began, leaning toward them. He spoke emphatically, and his manner turned serious. "If word ever got out, my office would swarm with refugees. This secret must remain here."

Still stunned, the twins nodded their agreement. "But . . . but where did you learn Serbian?" Voja asked. "You speak so fluently, like a native."

"My mother was of Serbian descent. She taught me as a child. My father's people came from Belgium," he explained. "I served 10 years in the American Embassy in Belgrade. I'd go to Bristol's Restaurant regularly and seek out university students, buy them lunch, and practice conversation with them." He leaned back, relaxed, appearing pleased to talk.

"And German? You don't speak it at all?" Cveja wanted to know.

"Oh no," the consul shook his head. "I won't learn it." He cocked his head and leaned forward again, resting his elbows on the table. Voja's file lay in front of him.

"Now let's move on to more important things," he said. In all the excitement the twins had almost forgotten the reason for their visit. The consul opened the file, and then looked up, staring at the two identical faces looking back at him. Waving a finger in the air between them, his eyes darted from one twin to the other. "OK, now. Which one of you is Vojislav?" He asked sheepishly.

"That's me," Voja responded with a laugh. It was the twins' turn to be amused. "I'm the original. I'm 10 minutes older. He's the carbon copy," he added, grinning.

"Goodness, but you sure do look alike! Even your voices sound the same," the consul replied, pausing. "Well, Vojislav, I have good news for you. Your documents have arrived. Washington has approved your application. You're going to America!"

Voja sat immobile. Had he heard right? Was his mind playing tricks? He turned to Cveja who was sitting bolt upright on the edge of his chair, beaming at him like a lantern. Yes, it was true. He was so overwhelmed he could not speak.

"Thank God!" Cveja exclaimed for him. "That's wonderful news!"

"But, but . . ." Voja stammered, finally regaining his voice. "What about my physical?"

"Ah, yes." The consul responded. He tapped his temple with his finger, and there was a hint of mischief in his smile. Turning to Cveja, he asked, "Did you bring your papers?"

Cveja handed him a large brown envelope.

Michelin reviewed its contents, looking pleased. "All the information here is exactly the same for both of you. Your date of birth, place of birth, address, physical description, parents' names, occupation, religion. Everything!" He pointed to the paper. "The only difference is your first names."

It was all beyond the twins' comprehension. Things had suddenly begun moving way too fast.

"To expedite matters, we'll make a copy of this document and then simply blot out *Svetozar* and insert *Vojislav*." He appraised Cveja. "And maybe change the weight." Since arriving in Austria almost emaciated, Cveja had put on 55 pounds. Now, he outweighed his brother.

"Vojislav, do you have any health problems?" he asked.

"None I know of."

"Just as I thought. A healthy Serbian specimen—you can't be much different than your twin." Then he rang for his secretary and handed her the documents with his instructions.

"The Pan American refugee flight leaves tomorrow, and you'll be on it," the consul announced, turning back to the twins. "It leaves from Munich at 7:00 p.m."

The twins exchanged stupefied glances. This was the last Pan American flight before Cveja's visa expired in eight days.

A short time later, the secretary returned with two sets of papers and two large envelopes. The consul perused them and put one set in one envelope. Handing it to Voja he said, "Here's your American visa and your documents." He put Cveja's documents in the other envelope and returned it to him.

"Take these envelopes to the refugee office at the World Council of Churches. They'll have your plane tickets and a few final papers to sign." He closed the file, letting his right hand fall with a thud as a gesture of finality. Again he smiled.

"Oh, one more thing," he said, raising his index finger as if the thought had just occurred to him. "Let me call Pan American to be sure there are seats." He picked up the phone, and the twins exchanged another astonished glance. Things were moving so fast now it took their breath away.

"You just made it!" the consul said, hanging up the receiver. "There were just three seats left. I reserved two for you." Then he stood up, shook their hands vigorously, and wished them well. "Let me know how you make out in America," he said, escorting them out of the room.

"Mr. Michelin," Voja stopped at the door and turned. "There's something I'd like to know. It's about my accuser."

Michelin smiled understandingly. "I'm afraid I can't tell you. That information is confidential, of course." He put his hand on Voja's shoulder and looked him in the eye. "Anyway, what good would it do for you to know? Sometimes people who are rejected take their frustration out on someone else. Who knows why people do what they do? Anyway, *Božja je osveta* [Vengeance is God's]."

They shook hands again, and the twins, carrying their precious papers, floated down the stairs, past the receptionist, and out of the building.

It was a two-mile walk to the refugee office. For the first time in two weeks, the winter sun shone. The streets and walks had been cleared of snow except for a thin, dry layer that stubbornly adhered to the ground and crunched under the rubber treads of their shoes. Hardly speaking as they walked, the twins tossed each other bewildered glances and occasional giddy smiles, and they couldn't stop shaking their heads. Having waited nearly two years with their future in limbo, they were now groggy from the speed at which things had suddenly plunged ahead.

Arriving at the brown, barracks-type building, they opened the door and entered the open area inside. "I just got my visa! We're leaving tomorrow!" Voja announced to the surprised staff who instantly surrounded them, hurling questions from all sides.

Just then Boba emerged from his office. "Come in, come in. Tell me what happened," he said, shutting the door behind them. They sat across from his desk. "Voja, when did you have your physical?"

Voja shrugged his shoulders. "All I know is that everything has been completed, and I have all my papers," he replied.

"Perfect. The details, after all, are not important," Boba replied, smiling warmly. "You've waited a long time. I'm proud of you two boys. It's been a privilege to know you."

Voja recalled the report of Boba's heartfelt words which had prompted the consul to reconsider Voja's case. He wanted to express gratitude to Boba for his trust, but doing so would betray the confidence. In his heart he asked God to bless this noble man who had dedicated his life to serving others.

"When you get to America," Boba advised, "try to find work in your own field. Be willing to start at the bottom, no matter how low the pay. You can work your way up. And though you may prefer to speak Serbian—or any other language, for that matter—" he chuckled and looked at Cveja, "learn to speak English. You can if you try."

"Now, let me get your things." He left his office and returned after a few minutes with two small envelopes and two navy-blue canvas bags.

"Here are the papers you need for the flight. Show them to the immigration official at the airport," Boba instructed. He handed the twins the sealed envelopes. "These contain your plane tickets and World Council of Churches identification badges with your name. And these bags will identify you as part of the refugee group." He held up the bags emblazoned *WCC* on the side in light blue. Then he stood up, held out his hands, and embraced the twins. With hearts overflowing with gratitude too deep to express, they thanked him for everything he had done for them. The specifics remained unsaid.

As soon as they reached home, they dashed into Pastor Schnötzinger's office to tell him the good news. *"Gott sei dank* [Thank God]!" he shouted. He jumped up and hugged them. When the twins returned to their apartment, they began packing their clothes and preparing to vacate the apartment. The rest of the day was spent saying goodbye to the people in the building.

News of the twins' imminent departure spread rapidly. Church members living in the neighborhood dropped by with good wishes, hugs, and small gifts—a pen, a box of stationery, a piece of homemade apple strudel for their trip. After two years of waiting, the time had come to move on.

CHAPTER 20

DATE WITH DESTINY

Voja awoke early the next morning to the clacking of diesel engines and the whistling and rumbling of trucks. It was Wednesday, January 28, 1959, and he and his brother had a date with destiny.

Jumping out of bed he dashed to the window and pulled aside the curtains. The air outside looked frigid and foggy, and the windowsill was lined with snow. More of the fluffy white stuff edged the railing on their balcony and blanketed the rooftops. Ice glittered like silver jewels on the bare branches of the chestnut and sycamore trees below.

"Just what we needed, snow!" he grumbled to himself. He could hear snow plows down the street scraping and clearing away the snow, the trucks whistling and rumbling as they hauled it away. "I don't care what anybody says. Snow is *not* beautiful! I wouldn't want to be one of those trees!" He frowned, dropped the curtains back, and turned toward Cveja, who had just come back from the shower room wrapped in a bathrobe, a towel draped around his neck. "How cold does it get in New York City?" Voja asked.

"New York? Beats me," he shrugged. "No matter how cold it gets, it'll be America," Cveja replied unsympathetically.

As they placed their remaining belongings into their suitcases, they looked around the room in which they had received so many friends. They were packing up their lives and saying a final farewell again, this time to Europe. In Voja's suitcase lay an English tutorial, bruised and battered. Also tucked snugly in his bag was the picture from the Unpardonable Sin brochure and the out-of-focus snapshot he didn't like. He glanced at the picture again and smiled to himself, "My American chick."

"Are you ready?" Pastor Schnötzinger called out as he knocked at the door. On very short notice the families who worked and lived in the building had prepared a farewell reception for the twins in the fellowship hall of the church. Gathered around a long table, they reminisced as they shared their last meal together.

"*Du bist mein Strizi* [You are my rascal]," the pastor said to Voja. He waved a plump finger at Voja and laughed heartily. For almost two years, the pastor had been the dubious beneficiary of many of Voja's jokes. "Who will make me laugh when you're gone? And who will I tease when you're no longer here?" he asked, still laughing.

"*Und Du bist mein Sänger* [You are my singer]." The pastor turned to Cveja. He flung a chubby arm around Cveja's shoulder. "I will miss you and your singing. It blessed my heart."

The pastor had always been there when the twins needed help, and they had not let him down either. A deep bond of friendship had developed between the three men, and it was with great sadness that they anticipated the imminent separation.

Around 3:00 p.m., Pastor Schnötzinger led the twins outside the building to his Volkswagen Beetle. "We'll never fit," Voja whispered to Cveja as he eyed the car, the corpulent pastor, and his equally sizable daughter.

The pastor guessed at his concern. "Take a deep breath and don't let it out," he told them. Somehow they managed to squeeze in, the pastor and his daughter in front, Cveja and Voja in the back, and their suitcases in the trunk. This would be the twins' last trip in this car.

Two chartered Mercedes buses were waiting in front of the World Council of Churches building when the four arrived. Inside the immigration office, there was barely enough room for the many people milling about. Refugees from surrounding camps were saying their goodbyes and signing out on Boba's departure list. Some refugees, who had come to see others off, began to cry because they would never see America. For whatever reason, the United States had rejected their applications, and they were slated to go to other countries. Tears of joy and sadness flowed freely as friends embraced—those who had been helped and those who had helped them. In all probability they would never see each other again.

Eventually the refugees began to make their way outside, huddling together in small groups on the walkway. Boba, Ratko, and Duško stood in front of the door beside the twins, the pastor and his daughter beside them.

Staff members inside peered out through the cloudy window pane and waved. Pastor Schnötzinger bowed his head and led his little group in prayer. Then they embraced, said goodbye, and reluctantly broke away.

The group of red-eyed, sniffly refugees boarded the buses, which pulled away with a jumble of waving hands thrust out the windows. With well wishes ringing in their ears, cheeks wet with tears, fond faces etched in memory, and excitement in their hearts, the refugees began the first leg of their journey.

The heavy snowfall the night before had left many drifts. Most of the streets had been cleared, but the ones cluttered with snow slowed their progress. The 75-mile trip to Munich took more than two hours. Munich had been the capital of Bavaria since the 16th century and, in 1919, had given birth to what became the Nazi Party. Although World War II had ended 14 years earlier, some of the buildings still lay in ruins. As Voja peered out the window, he saw other buildings that were encrusted with scaffolding and appeared to be at various stages of restoration. Despite the bad weather, the buses arrived at Munich's International Airport with more than an hour to spare.

Voja, Cveja, and the other refugees spilled out of the buses with their meager belongings, following their leader into the terminal assigned to each bus group. After passing through Customs and Immigration to have their passports, vaccination documents, and other papers checked, they made their way to the gate and waited.

"Flight 800 to New York City now boarding at gate 10," the announcement in German finally blared over the loudspeaker. Voja's heart leaped with excitement. His palms were sweaty—he and Cveja were actually on their way to America.

Lining up with the nervous, strangely silent group, they waited to board the four-motor propeller plane. This was their first flight ever, and when everyone was finally settled on board, every seat was occupied.

After the preliminary announcements, the "Fasten Your Seat Belt" sign came on and the passengers obediently complied. Soon the engines roared, and the plane taxied slowly to the end of the runway. Then with full-throated thunder the aircraft lunged forward, pushing the twins back in their seats. The pilot turned the nose of the plane skyward, and they lifted off into the night sky. A few minutes later their world disappeared beneath the clouds.

Peering out the window through spaces in the clouds below, Voja spotted city lights scattered across the continent. The thought struck him that he was gliding smoothly above the turbulent weather and conflicting politics of the countries below. His fellow passengers appeared enraptured too and sat in a strange, benumbed silence, each one lost in his own thoughts. Only the steady drone of propellers and an occasional muffled voice or child's cry disrupted the eerie stillness. He leaned back, feeling wonderfully alive. He was saying goodbye to his old life—a new one awaited him on the other side of the ocean.

With few exceptions, the 120 people the plane accommodated were all refugees. Young and old, men, women, and little children—all bound for new homes in an alien land—seemed suspended in an unreal world, the past retreating below and the future unknown yet full of hope. What little most of them knew about America had been derived from their geography and history classes in school, from Radio Free Europe broadcasts, and from Hollywood movies with happy endings. Fantasies of freedom and hopes for a better life had led them to believe that in America, as movies depicted at that time, the good guys always won and crime never paid.

"There's a blizzard in Shannon, Ireland. The airport is closed," the pilot announced some time later. "We are being rerouted and will refuel in the Canary Islands." The cabin lights dimmed, and many of the passengers dozed off while others stared out the window into the dark.

When the plane landed in the Canaries at 2:00 a.m., Cveja and Voja stepped outside into balmy tropical breezes and swaying palm fronds. They were sure it was a dream—a dream from which they did not want to awaken.

Once they were back in the air again, Voja began reflecting on the events of the past two years. He turned to Cveja. "Remember that day in Kalemegdan Park?"

"How could I forget?" Cveja replied. He was wide awake and reclining in his seat, a pillow behind his head. His thoughts quickly retreated to that spring day when he and Voja had tasted the first real pledge of freedom, captured God's promise in the Bible, and watched the flight of the gray falcon.

Voja stared out the window into the darkness. Far below, now black with night, lay the vast Atlantic Ocean. He thought of how freely its waters moved, how effortlessly cruise ships and transports crisscrossed its waterways to the far ends of the world. And up here in the atmosphere, the plane soared easily through the air. The engine ground on noisily as the aircraft rode the currents of the wind—the twins' own gray falcon, huge and strong, carrying them to freedom. They were a part of it now, moving freely already.

"So many things have happened since then," he mused aloud. "So many coincidences."

"Yes. Both strange and fascinating, wonderfully woven together," Cveja replied. "It's incredible how God brought everything together and worked out our problems."

"Like when my name was listed for the trip to Rome," Voja said almost reverently. "And when the American Consul confided in Boba. He took a big risk rushing my papers through. And Boba, what moved him to say those words? That made the difference for me."

"It sure did. He is a great man." Cveja looked over at his brother. "I could have been arrested several times, but I wasn't. I could even have been killed!" He paused, remembering. "The bus accident saved me from going to prison with the group I missed."

"And if that lady in Rijeka hadn't looked up Bartoni's file and found out he worked with the police, you wouldn't be here," Voja added. "I wouldn't be here either, if you had taken that other job in Salzburg."

The two men fell silent and closed their tired eyes. Before long the eastern sky began to brighten as a new day dawned.

"Due to a heavy snow fall, Idlewild Airport [renamed JFK Airport in 1963] on Long Island has closed," the pilot said over the loudspeaker some time later. "We'll have to reroute to Gander, Newfoundland. We'll wait there until we're cleared to continue." The announcement woke the twins from their slumber.

"Oooooh," a low moan signaled the disappointment of the few passengers who understood English. Immediately, muffled questions sputtered across the cabin in both Hungarian and Serbo-Croatian. "What did he say? What did he say?" By now Voja's English had improved somewhat and by confering with one of the other refugees, he was able to figure out the message. Soon the plane landed in Gander where they waited for the signal to take to the air again.

Three hours into the final leg of the flight, a bell rang and the "Fasten Your Seat Belt" and "No Smoking" signs came on. Voja felt the nose of the plane dip downward. The flight attendants walked through, and the plane began its slow descent. Everyone on board was now wide awake and eager, and the air practically buzzed with excitement.

"We'll soon see Manhattan Island." At the pilot's announcement, all heads jerked toward the windows. The word "Manhattan" was unmistakable. The refugees peered out the windows, craning their necks from one side to the other in an effort to catch a glimpse of New York City.

Drifting downward, the plane banked sharply over New York Harbor and someone shouted, "The Statue of Liberty!" All eyes turned toward the windows on that side. Down below on Liberty Island, Lady Liberty stood tall, holding her beacon high to welcome the weary masses who hungered to be free. At the sight of her welcoming torch the passengers burst into wild applause and loud cheering.

But there was another lady in New York whom Voja hoped would welcome him. A lady he had kept waiting too long. *What would she be like?* he wondered. *Was it meant to be? Would she be waiting still? Had she waited at all?*

Their eyes glued to the window, the twins devoured every detail as they surveyed the land that would be their future home. They didn't want to miss the landmarks they had studied about in school—this was a preview of the life they would soon begin. Below they saw a strange new concrete city, Manhattan Island, a jungle of glass, steel, and concrete. Above the tall spires rose the Empire State Building, the tallest building in the world at that time.

"Down there is the most expensive park in the world," the pilot announced, as they flew over Central Park in the middle of Manhattan Island. The passengers peered down at the long green rectangle dotted with blue lakes and flanked by buildings that seemed to reach up to the clouds. The pilot banked right and turned toward Long Island.

"On the right side you can see Brooklyn Bridge!" the pilot indicated. "It's not for sale today," he joked.

Nearly 24 hours after departing from Munich, the plane touched down at Idlewild Airport. There, in the last two of three seats available, on the last refugee flight out before Cveja's visa expired forever, the twins arrived at their dream destination.

"Welcome to America!" the pilot said when the plane stopped at the gate. The twins exchanged eager glances. That welcome included them. It had been a long flight with several detours, just like their personal journeys. They felt as though they had traveled a million miles. And at 11:30 a.m. on Thursday, January 29, 1959, Voja and Cveja stepped onto American soil.

Outside the day looked as gray as the one they had left behind. The runways had been cleared of snow but there was snow piled up everywhere else. The glass and steel airport buildings and tower were much the same as any other large airport. But the twins were in America now, where all things are possible and dreams come true. All the disappointments and trials that had led them to this place, all the scrambled pieces of the puzzle, had come together to form a picture which bore the imprint of God.

CHAPTER 21

VOJA MEETS THE "UNPARDONABLE SIN"

Inside Idlewild Airport, it took some time for the twins' documents and baggage to be processed through Customs and Immigration. When Voja and Cveja finally emerged, they found their friend Mladen waiting. After the airline had announced the plane's delays, he had gone home during the interim and returned in time for the newly scheduled arrival. On the drive to Mladen's apartment in his 1957 Plymouth, there was much to talk about.

It was almost two o'clock in the afternoon when the three men climbed up the stairs and entered Mladen's second-floor Jackson Heights apartment and found Mela and the couple's four children waiting to give them a hearty welcome. Mirjana and Nevenka, the two oldest girls whom Voja had babysat after the couple left the country, were now 12 and 10 years old. Although they were older now, they were still petite. The two younger children, a girl, Nadica, and a boy, Djordje, were now 3 years old and 13 months of age respectively.

The fragrant odors of *gibanica* and stuffed cabbage swirled around the small kitchen as the family and their guests caught up on old times while Mela set the table for dinner. "Do you remember when I took you to the field near your grandmother's house and you slid down the haystacks?" Voja asked the older girls, attempting to reconnect with them.

"Yeah, that was so much fun!" Mirjana, the eldest, replied enthusiastically.

"You were always teasing us and telling us stories," Nevenka said. *"Daj moju djigericu!"* she shouted in a deep, gruff voice, imitating Voja's rendition. After whispering a scary story to them, he would conclude with the loud demand: "Give me my liver!" And the two girls would squeal with laughter. "That story scared us to pieces!" Nevenka added. "But we loved to hear you tell it!"

They laughed and talked over dinner, recalling happy days in Belgrade. The jovial couple's former home in Belgrade had been a haven for the students who often gathered there. The twins had many times enjoyed the couple's hospitality and Mela's exceptional cooking.

By the time the group finished eating, the clock showed 4:00 p.m. Daylight had already begun to wash out of the sky as the sun dropped toward the horizon. The days were short now in the middle of winter. The yawning twins, exhausted by their long trip and unaccustomed to the seven-hour time difference, were ready for bed.

In one of the two bedrooms, a bed sheet hanging from a rod divided it in two compartments. The two older girls slept on one side, and the twins slept on the other. Mladen, Mela, and their two smaller children slept in the second bedroom. It was tight quarters, but a welcome beginning for the twins until they could find jobs and rent their own place.

But the question pressing on Voja's mind would not rest. Before retiring for the night, he had to get an answer. "Mela, what kind of snapshot did you send me of that girl? She's not nice looking at all," he said.

"What snapshot? Oh, you mean the one Mladen took?" She waved her hand and laughed. "Nobody looks good in *his* pictures. Don't you know that? Anyway, Voja, you'll see her in church."

The next morning when they awoke, Mladen had already left for work. His printing job on Long Island meant a long commute. Mirjana was using the only bathroom, and Nevenka waited her turn. "You're after Nevenka," Mela said to the twins, laughing good-naturedly. "We have to wait in line, like we did during occupation times. Hitler taught us to be patient." She laughed again.

Once breakfast was over and the two older girls left for school, Mela puttered around the house and prepared to go grocery shopping. "Today you'll see what food markets look like in America," she said. She piled Nadica and Djordje into a folding stroller, and they set out to walk to the store.

Upon entering the food market, the twins' eyes grew large. The sight of shelves stocked full with colorfully packaged goods of all types, every department abounding with variety, and all kinds of fresh produce in the dead of winter, left them looking on in awe. "Austria has its grocery stores, France has its large markets, but nothing compares with this!" Cveja exclaimed. "You even have oranges in January!"

Mela took the children out of the stroller and put them in one of the store's shopping carts, then hung the folded stroller on the front of the cart.

Cveja took another shopping cart, since they were not large, and they started down the aisles. After selecting a large turkey to roast for Sabbath dinner, some salad makings from the produce section, and several other things on her shopping list, Mela, her brood, and her guests headed home.

When they arrived at the apartment, Mladen was already there. On Fridays his work let out at noon. At that time of day, traffic on the Grand Central Parkway was light so his commute was relatively short. "Hey, Mela, give me something to eat. I'm about ready to gnaw at the table," he wailed impatiently.

"Mladen, you'll have to wait," she said as she hurried to prepare lunch.

After they sat down at the table, Mladen thanked the Lord for His bounties and for the safe arrival of their friends. "Eat, eat!" Mela urged her two older daughters when she saw them picking at their food. "Look how skinny you are! If you want to look nice like Ena, you've got to eat," Mela laughed.

Since Mela had brought up Ann's name, Voja quickly asked Mladen about the girl who had long occupied his thoughts. "That brochure you sent, 'The Unpardonable Sin,' showed a picture of a girl," Voja said, switching the conversation deftly.

"You want to see her, don't you?" Mladen said tauntingly. "Just remember. She's a fine girl, quite serious. So be careful how you behave, you rascal," he chuckled.

"So you want to see Ena?" the older girls echoed.

"Yes, I do!" Voja said emphatically. He smiled and said, "So what?"

The next day was Sabbath. Voja and Cveja got up early to avoid waiting in line for the washroom, but they were still groggy as their bodies had not yet adjusted to Eastern Standard Time. The others arose later to prepare for church.

After breakfast, the two older girls squeezed into the front seat of the family car with their parents, while the two little ones sat on the twins' laps in the back seat. Then they set out for the half hour drive to Astoria, to the first Yugoslavian Seventh-day Adventist Church built in America.

As they neared the church, both girls suddenly cried out in unison. "Look, there she is!" They pointed to the car that had just turned into their lane in front of them.

"Who?" Voja asked.

"Ena! The girl you want to meet!" Mirjana said excitedly.

"Who else would we be talking about?" Nevenka added with a hint of indignation in her voice.

Voja stared into the back of the car. There in the back seat sat a girl with dark, wavy, shoulder-length hair. Two older people, apparently her parents, sat on either side.

"It's Pastor Kanachky's car," Mladen explained. "He often picks them up and brings them to church so they don't have to use the bus. Her mother's health is frail."

As Voja watched, the pastor's car turned onto 32nd Street and parked in a space reserved for the pastor at the curb in front of the church. There was no parking lot since most people didn't have a car and traveled by public transportation. Mladen followed and stopped his car just behind the pastor's to let out his family. Cveja and Voja started to leave.

"Hey, not you, Voja," Mladen said, laughing. "You're coming with me." He drove around the corner to find another parking spot on the street. By the time Mladen and Voja walked back to the church, the family had already gone inside.

Mladen preceded Voja up the concrete stairs of the attractive little church sandwiched between two brick buildings. Inside the vestibule several people stood talking quietly. Cveja, Mela, and the two girls had hung up their coats on the coat rack and were divesting the little ones of their winter wear. To the side of the little group, the girl with the dark brown hair stood with her back to them.

Voja felt his heart race with expectation. She had removed her coat, and he could see her tall, slender form. After all this time, he was about to meet his Unpardonable Sin, the girl whose picture he had been talking to for months. But the image on the out-of-focus snapshot haunted his mind, and though eager, he feared disappointment.

"Well here we are," Mladen announced, in a move to draw attention. Suddenly the girl turned around, and Voja recognized the dark eyes and arched brows that he had so carefully scrutinized under the magnifying glass with Adolf so many months before. His fears dissolved into great relief, and when she smiled at him the image on the snapshot vanished into nothingness. He thought she looked even better in person than the picture on the brochure. A joy he had never felt before flooded his being. That moment, Voja made a decision: this was the girl of his dreams, and she would one day be his wife.

"The twins finally arrived," Mladen said, and then introduced Voja and Cveja to the group. Voja and Ann exchanged a few words, and then she disappeared into the sanctuary. Moments later, sweet piano music floated out to the vestibule. Ann was playing the piano in preparation for Sabbath School to begin.

After the mission story Mladen announced to the church that after a long wait, the young men had finally arrived, and he hoped everyone would get to know them. While the twins had been waiting in Austria, he had given the church members general updates on the progress of their papers. That was all Ann knew of the twins. She had no idea of Voja's claim on her, much less that there were people who knew her as "The Unpardonable Sin."

When she played the small Hammond organ later for the worship service, Voja sat entranced. It was a simple hymn played by an average organist on a basic organ. But he felt like he had ascended to heaven, and "The Unpardonable Sin" was his angel. After church let out, the members gathered around to welcome the twins, and then they all dispersed to their homes.

"So how do you like her?" Mirjana and Nevenka assailed Voja in the car on the drive home.

"Hey, nothing special!" he responded, anticipating their spirited reaction.

"Nothing special? Nothing special?" the girls chorused.

"Who do you think you are? Some kind of Prince Charming or something?" Mirjana demanded.

"Yeah, what did you expect?" Nevenka added. Accustomed to his teasing, they had learned to be feisty. Mela and Mladen laughed at the banter. Cveja eyed his brother, amused but wondering. As soon as they walked into the apartment, Mladen pulled Voja aside and asked, "OK, so what do you really think?"

"Not bad," Voja replied matter-of-factly.

But Mladen was onto him. "You Šabac rascal you," he laughed. "I know you better than that!"

CHAPTER 22

NEW BEGINNINGS

Monday morning, Pastor Kanachky arrived at Mladen's house with a copy of the help wanted section of Sunday's The New York *Times*. He had spotted several ads in the paper for architects and draftsmen and had come to help the twins find jobs. Consulting with the pastor about the ads, they chose several to reply to and he phoned for appointments.

The first appointment was at 1:00 that afternoon. After a half hour subway ride in non-rush hour traffic they arrived on the east side of Manhattan to make their first call. At the front desk the pastor introduced himself and the twins and told the receptionist of their appointment with the personnel director. Shortly afterward a gentleman came out to meet them.

"I'm Pastor Kanachky. These two young men are architects. They came from Europe, and they're looking for jobs." He introduced the twins by name as they shook hands with the interviewer.

After seating them in his office, the man asked his first question: "Do they have any American experience?"

"Unfortunately they don't," the pastor replied. "They just arrived. But they have worked as architects in Yugoslavia and Austria."

"What about their drawings? Have they any samples to show me?" the man then asked.

The pastor looked at the twins, who shook their heads. All their drawings had remained behind in Europe.

"I'm sorry," the man said. "If you can bring us some drawings, we'd be happy to discuss this further." After shaking hands with the interviewer again, the twins and the pastor left.

After three such experiences during the first week of searching for a job, they noticed that the architects in these offices drew their plans in pencil.

The twins had learned to draw in black ink, which was more precise but also more difficult and did not allow for correction. Voja decided to replicate from memory the floor plan and elevation of a church for which he had drawn plans in Yugoslavia. The pastor offered him the use of the drawing table which he used to lay out graphics for the religious brochures he printed, one of which was Voja's cherished "Unpardonable Sin."

At the pastor's house the next week, Voja began. He drew the plan in metric 1 to 100 scale, which closely approximated 1/8" scale (1 to 96). He penciled in the lines and then drew over them in black ink with a Feder pen, something American architects were not usually trained to do. Thanks to the photographic memory with which he and his brother were endowed, it was not difficult to reproduce the plan. By the end of the week, it was finished.

When they made their calls the following week, they carried the rolled-up drawing with them. Everyone who saw it was impressed. But having solved the first problem, they were confronted with another. "How good is their English?" the interviewers would ask the pastor. In response Voja would slip behind the pastor and Cveja behind him.

Every evening the twins watched television to acclimate their ears to the sounds of the American-style English language, so they could learn to decipher the words. Wherever they went now, they kept their ears open to catch snatches of conversations. The exposure helped immensely. Even Cveja, faced now with the reality of earning a living in America, made serious attempts to improve his knowledge of English.

Ika, a new acquaintance whom they had met through friends, referred the brothers to Eggers & Higgins, where a Serbian friend of his worked in the personnel office. The architectural firm, second largest in America at the time, employed 400 architects and support staff in two offices. The main office, located on 42nd Street across from Grand Central Station, occupied two floors. So during their fourth week in America, the twins, accompanied by the pastor, set out to put in applications.

After talking for a while, the Serb led the three men to the office of the chief draftsman for an interview. "If he's interested in you," he told the twins, "he'll consult with one of the partners."

In the chief draftsman's office, Voja unrolled his drawing on the desk, and the man immediately reacted. "This is excellent!" He examined the details. "Very precise," he continued as he inspected the drawing for several minutes. Then he rolled it up and turned to the twins. "I'm impressed," he exclaimed. In the conversation that followed he learned more about the twins and then spoke about himself.

"My father came from Hungary before I was born, so I understand what it's like for an immigrant. It's hard to adjust to a new country," he said. "But I need to hear your English." Those fateful words again.

"I can spell 3,000 words," Voja told him, speaking with a heavy accent, "but I need to improve my pronunciation." The man smiled, spoke with Cveja, and then excused himself, carrying the drawing with him to the office of one of the partners. It just so happened that the two Eggers brothers who owned the firm were identical twins. A few minutes later he returned, smiling.

"Yes, we will hire you. It will be on a probationary basis for six months," he said to the twins' immense relief and great joy. "Voja will work here, in the main office, since his English is somewhat better, and Cveja will go to our branch office. It's on First Avenue across from the United Nations Building. You may both start on Monday."

Elated, the twins and the pastor left. Just as Boba in the refugee office and the American Consul in Salzburg had urged them to do, they had each found a job in their own field, although on probation and starting at the bottom of the pay scale. Many highly-trained immigrants such as medical doctors, lawyers, and engineers settled for whatever job they could get in order to survive. Only one month had passed since arriving in America, and they felt a new confidence that they could work their way up.

With the job situation settled, they signed up at a local high school for evening classes in English conversation. There they met others like themselves who struggled with the English language but who persevered because they wanted to become Americans.

The first day at work in the main office, Voja realized he'd have to change the spelling of his name from Voja to Voya because Americans pronounced the "j" hard, as in Jeff, making his name VOH-dja. Henceforth, he would spell his name Voya. He also changed the spelling of his last name to Vitorovich.

The chief draftsman took Voya to meet the man who would be his supervisor. "This is Roland, and this is Voya," he said, introducing the two men. Of all places, Roland was from Alabama, and he spoke with a deep southern drawl, something Voya had never heard before. Showing Voya to a drafting table which would be his work base, Roland laid out a drawing on the board and began giving him instructions.

"Wherrlewherrrrelwall stair. Whiiirrrolaajm scale. Whreelkwahalal enlarge. Do y'all unduhstayand?" he asked.

Voya shook his head. "No. I'm sorry," he said. He felt like he was back in Salzburg listening to the American Consul speak English, only now, instead of picking out every twentieth word, he understood every fifth. Not nearly enough to hold down a job.

During the interchange with Roland, Voya noticed the man at the drafting table in front of him occasionally turning around to listen. As soon as Voya said he didn't understand, the man spoke up. *"Entschuldiegen, sprechen sie doch Deutsch* [Excuse me, but do you speak German]?" he asked, his German flavored with an Austrian accent. It seemed to Voya that the sun suddenly broke through dark, dismal clouds, brightening his whole day.

"Why, yes, I speak German fluently," Voya replied eagerly in German.

"Wait a moment," the man said and came over. He introduced himself to Voya as Ali and asked Roland to repeat the instructions to him. As he did so, Voya strained to understand his speech. This time he recognized a few more English words in addition to every German word of Ali's.

"Did you bring your drafting tools?" Ali asked Voya, after repeating Roland's instructions to him. Voya pulled out his metric tools. "Oh, no, we don't use the metric system here," he said. "We use inches and feet in America."

Voya looked puzzled. He knew nothing of inches or feet.

"In what scale is this drawing?" Ali asked of the drawing Voya was to work from to see if he could figure it out.

"It looks to me like metric 1 to 200," Voya replied, as they continued conversing in German.

"You're right, Voya," Ali said. "In metric it would be 1 to 192. This drawing is in 1/16-inch scale—1/16-inch equals one foot."

Voya looked blank.

"Don't worry, you'll catch on," Ali said. "I have an extra set of tools you can use."

Voya's first assignment consisted of drawing cross and longitudinal sections of a stairway for a 55-story skyscraper, enlarged from 1/16-inch to 1/4-

inch scale. "If you have any questions, feel free to ask me. I'll be glad to help," offered his new friend Ali.

For several months thereafter, whenever Voya ran into a problem or had a question, Ali was always there. In the course of time, Voya learned that Ali was a Jew from Vienna. In 1938, as things were heating up in Europe, his family waited for their passports to arrive so they could leave Austria for America. Ali's passport came first and, since he was of military age, his parents urged him to go on ahead. They would follow as soon as their documents arrived. As it turned out, their documents never came. Ali's family never made it to America. Soon afterward, the Nazis rounded them up and transported them to Dachau where they all died.

Meanwhile in the other office, Cveja found his name being pronounced KVE-dja instead of TSVE-ya, so he decided to Americanize it. Henceforth, he would be known as Steve, close enough to Svetozar, his full first name. Luckily for him, he met a Jewish architect fluent in French who helped him when he needed clarification. Once a week or so, Steve made a delivery to the main office, a walk of about one mile. Most people in the bustling main office were unaware that Voya had a twin.

One day when Steve made his delivery to the main office, one of the project architects who worked at the other end of the floor from Voya, gave Steve a set of drawings to take back to the branch office. He told him it was urgent and needed to be delivered immediately. Steve left right away.

About twenty minutes later, the man happened to pass by Voya's desk, noticing him for the first time and assuming he was Steve. Flustered and angry, he stormed into the chief draftsman's office to complain.

"I can't believe this foreigner. I gave him a set of drawings to take to the other office and told him it was urgent!" he fumed, pacing and waving his arms about. "That was twenty minutes ago, and I just saw him. He's still sitting here, without a care in the world!"

"So you mean to say he's still here? He never left?" The chief draftsman replied calmly, playing along. He was a bit of a joker and caught onto the situation immediately.

"Yeah! Yeah! That's what I said! He's just sitting there doing . . . I don't know what!" He waved his hands again and pouted. "What are you going to do about it?" he demanded.

"Not a thing," the chief draftsman replied. He pursed his lips and shook his head as he fiddled with his pencil. And then he grinned. "There are two of them. They're twins," he blurted out.

"Twins? You mean this foreigner has a brother?"

"Identical. The other one works in the branch office. If it will make you feel any better, call there to see if the drawings arrived."

The project architect picked up the phone on the desk and made the call. The plans had been delivered. A much calmer and happier man walked out of the chief draftsman's office.

Another day, just as Steve arrived at the main office, he heard another one of the project architects' angry outbursts for the first time. O'Malley was taking out his ire on his assistant, who remained sullen and silent. "There, you did it again! I can't believe you're so stupid!" he ranted. In the open-floor office, everyone easily heard the harangue, but hardly anyone paid attention anymore to the man's regular displays of temper.

"Fix this thing!" O'Malley demanded of his assistant. The wire on the parallel bar of his drafting board had broken. Frustrated and impatient, he was unable to install the new wire himself.

"I don't know how," the assistant replied meekly.

"You don't know how," the project architect mimicked his words and grimaced. "I can't believe you're so dumb!"

"Well, if *you're* so smart, how come *you* can't fix it yourself?" the assistant unexpectedly snapped back.

"Oooooooooh!" a chorus crescendoed across the floor like a tidal wave, as surprised employees lifted their heads and grinned with amusement. This was the first time the assistant had barked back at his boss, who stood stunned, his eyes blazing.

Disturbed by what he had just heard, Steve approached Voya's desk. "I know how to change the wire. Maybe I should help," he said, speaking in Serbian.

"Are you kidding? Stay away," Voya warned his brother sternly. "It's not your problem." Being the elder twin, Voya expected his brother to heed his advice. But Steve walked toward the still-fuming O'Malley in total disregard of his admonition.

"What do *you* want?" the man sputtered at Steve when he noticed him approaching.

"Mr. O'Malley, I can help. I can fix wire," Steve said eagerly, but with a decided accent.

"You! Why you can't even speak English," O'Malley retorted. "Who *are* you, anyway?"

"My name Svetozar Vitorovic. Call me Steve. I work in other office," he said with a shy smile as he proceeded to bend over the man's drafting table.

Striking his usual authoritative stance with his fists planted on his portly hips, O'Malley watched as Steve removed the screws on the parallel bar, pulled out the broken wire, carefully threaded the new wire into the parallel and around the board, and tightened it. Then he moved the parallel up and down to test it. Satisfied that it worked, he straightened up and grinned. "There, Mr. O'Malley, it's fixed."

"Well, well, well!" the man bellowed as he scrutinized the foreigner. He looked both pleased and surprised. "I tell you what," he said after a moment's reflection, "to show my appreciation, I'm going to ask that you be assigned to my group."

The man's words sent muffled snickers skittering across the floor. Assignment to O'Malley's group was dreaded by every architect in the office who had been around long enough to know. What Steve viewed as a reward, the others saw as severe punishment.

Sitting at his drafting desk about 30 feet away, Voya shook his head and sent Steve an I-warned-you-but-you-wouldn't-listen look as O'Malley bounded toward one of the partner's offices at the other end of the floor and disappeared inside.

From somewhere on the floor a voice called out, "So much for being a good Samaritan," and laughter rippled through the room. One architect came up to Steve and said sympathetically, "You don't know what you're getting yourself into. The man is a terror."

Soon a grinning O'Malley returned and walked straight toward Steve, who was about to return to the branch office. "OK, it's official. You start with me two weeks from Monday," he announced proudly.

On their way home, Voya proceeded to warn Steve about O'Malley's reputation, and Steve vowed to do his best. He spent a lot of time asking God for patience and the willingness to do whatever it took to please his boss.

Two weeks later, Steve moved to the main office and joined the group of seven architects over which O'Malley presided. From where he sat, Voya could see the group. All that week he observed Steve cheerfully going about his work. When O'Malley appeared impatient, Steve quickly offered to help. When O'-Malley began to growl because his assistant mixed up the shop drawings for the Baptist church on which they were working, Steve helped reconcile the problem. The shop drawings for the stained glass windows from Paris were in metric measurements and written in French, and Steve knew both.

"What would I do without you, Steve?" O'Malley was often heard to say. He loved Steve's approach and input, and Steve quickly gained his confidence.

When Steve asked O'Malley for permission to leave early on Fridays in order to observe his Sabbath, O'Malley immediately agreed. "How can I say no to you?" he said.

"You can't!" rang out a brave voice from somewhere close enough to hear but far enough away to remain anonymous.

"You're lucky to have him!" another chimed in.

"Just be sure you make up the time," O'Malley replied to Steve, ignoring the remarks.

In the meantime, many things were happening in the twins' personal lives. Voya and Ann saw each other in church each week and began accompanying the pastor and his wife on their weekly drive after Sabbath service to Elizabeth, New Jersey, where the pastor preached to another small congregation of Yugoslavs. On the way there they ate their sack lunches in the car. Each trip offered an opportunity to get better acquainted. Steve did not go.

The day Voya received his first paycheck he asked Ann out on their first date and brought her a small New York City souvenir gift. Since their work places were just half a mile apart, they began meeting briefly during their lunch break.

Three months after arriving in New York, Voya and Steve moved out of Mladen's house and rented their own one-bedroom apartment, also in Jackson Heights. When Voya accompanied Ann home after work on the subway, he occasionally stayed for dinner. Afterward he walked the two-plus miles home because subway trains ran infrequently in the evening and no direct bus service existed between the two places.

On May 17, about three and a half months after they first met, Voya and Ann were engaged. Since Ann did not wear jewelry, Voya gave her a beautiful diamond Longines watch engraved with a message of love on the back.

When the twins' six-month probation period at work ended, they were accepted as permanent employees and their salaries were increased. They kept studying diligently, and their English continued to improve.

Nearly seven months from the day Voya stepped off the plane and set foot on American soil, he and his "Unpardonable Sin" were married. "I came to America for freedom and lost it when I got married," he pretended to complain. On Sunday, August 16, the hottest day of the year, with the temperature topping 102 degrees, Pastor Kanachky performed the wedding in the Yugoslavian Seventh-day Adventist Church in Astoria. Though small and lacking air conditioning, it was the church which Ann's parents had helped to build, where she had been baptized, and where she and Voja first met face to face. A dinner reception at a nearby restaurant followed the wedding ceremony, and the couple honeymooned on St. Thomas in the Virgin Islands.

But there was another watch that Voya bought with his brother Steve, a gold Longines which they mailed to Boba, the director of the refugee center of the World Council of Churches in Salzburg. It was a token of their profound appreciation for all he had done for them. Shortly thereafter though, the watch came back with a note of appreciation for the thought. A most honorable man, Boba would not accept any reward for his work.

In the meantime Steve had started dating an American girl named Diana whose father came from Dalmatia, in Yugoslavia. Her mother was of Croatian descent and had been born in America. Diana had a beautiful dramatic soprano voice, and the couple often sang solos and duets at various churches in the city. In June of the following year, they married in an English-speaking Adventist church in Jackson Heights.

Meanwhile at work, O'Malley's temper still flared, but not nearly as often as before, and seldom at Steve. When the Baptist church project was completed after a year, leaving Steve free to leave, O'Malley asked him to stay on in his group for the next project. Steve agreed. He had discovered the decent person hidden beneath the blustery exterior. Nothing was too hard for him to do for the boss of whom he had grown very fond.

In December of 1960, Nata, Mica, and Jovica immigrated to the United States. Surprisingly, Nata had been able to get another visitor's visa to Salzburg, sponsored again by Walter and his wife. This time she came with Jovica. With the help of Pop Duško, a Serbian Orthodox priest who worked with the refugee office and had connections in Vienna, her visitor's visa was extended several times for more than a year while she waited for Mica to escape.

Just days before her last visa extension expired, Mica arrived. He had traveled by freight train from Belgrade to Slovenia to meet a guide. En route, he had hidden in the brake cabin of one of the freight cars. A conductor returning there after making his rounds discovered him. Since Mica knew that UDBA agents often boarded trains to track down stowaways, he acted as if he were on official police business and briskly waved the man away. Falling for his ruse, the conductor quickly left. Later the Slovenian guide took Mica across the border into Austria.

Once Mica finally arrived, Austria granted him and his little family political asylum. They would not give it to Nata without her husband. Their papers were processed rapidly, and the family soon came to America. In New York City, Mica started up his own painting and decorating business with good success. Jovica quickly learned English, and whenever he encountered a problem, he crossed the street and knocked on his Aunt Ann's door.

In 1961, Voya and Ann traveled to Europe intending to visit his mother. Because he had not served in the army, Voya could not risk entering Yugoslavia for fear he might be detained. Not yet an American citizen, he traveled with a Travel Document in Lieu of Passport. If the Communists forcibly kept him to serve in the military, it would jeopardize his permanent residency status and his pending American citizenship. So he waited in Salzburg, visiting with his friends Boba, Duško, and Ratko in the refugee office, and with members at church, while Ann took the Orient Express train to Belgrade to meet his mother and family in Glušci.

Voya's mother had been granted a passport which would allow her to go to Salzburg to see her son. That had been the plan when Voya and Ann initiated the trip. But the moment Ann crossed the border into Yugoslavia, the Communist government withdrew his mother's passport so she could not leave the country.

The next year, in 1962, Voya became a naturalized American citizen, his residency requirement reduced to three years because he was married to an American citizen. The first thing he did as a citizen was to submit a formal request to have his mother immigrate to America. When she came, the twins showed her around Manhattan Island and took her to see all the amazing sights. Having never ventured far from her village, the simple woman was overwhelmed with the wonders of her new world.

An interesting incident occurred while the twins worked at Eggers & Higgins. They were assigned to draw plans for the American Embassy in Ankara, Turkey. The general contractor for construction was a German firm, the contractor for interior decoration was a French firm, and the subcontractor for terrazzo flooring was an Italian firm in Rome. Since Voya and Steve knew the metric system and between them spoke German, French, and Italian, it was a perfect fit. The only problem was the required security clearance. When officials in Washington learned that two architects from Communist Yugoslavia would work on the highly confidential plans, they sent a government agent to investigate. One of the partners, David Eggers, who was a Roman Catholic, informed the agent that the twins did not need security clearance because they were Seventh-day Adventist Christians and the firm would guarantee for them. The twins learned about this later.

After seven years with this firm, Voja and Steve decided to leave. Of those seven years, Steve had spent four working with O'Malley. Even afterward, Steve and O'Malley kept in touch with occasional phone calls and cards. When O'Malley passed away some time later, his wife invited Steve to the private family funeral service as requested by O'Malley prior to his death.

At their new job at Welton Becket, another architectural firm in Manhattan, the twins worked as job captains. Each had charge of a project and supervised five or six architects. Along with the American architects in their groups were a Japanese, an Austrian, a Philippino lady, a South American, and two Turks—one Turk in each of their groups.

One day at lunchtime, as Steve sat in Voya's office, the two Turkish architects entered. One held a large tray covered with a lacy cloth. "Brothers Serb, what day is today?" he asked.

The twins shot each other a quick glance. It was June 28, Vidovdan, the anniversary of the Battle of Kosovo, made sacred by the sacrifice of the greatly outnumbered Serb army who fought against the invading Ottoman Turks to defend their country, freedom, and Christian faith. Not knowing what these men had in mind, Voya asked, "What day do you think it is?"

"Vidovdan! The Battle of Kosovo!" they replied. "And we have a gift for you, a peace offering. My sister brought it from Istanbul when she came to visit recently," the architect from Voya's group said, uncovering the tray of baklava.

"We knew you were Serbs when we first started working with you, and we worried what your attitude would be toward us," the other Turk said. "But you both have been very fair. Whenever we couldn't express ourselves in English, you helped by explaining things to us in German." These Turks had lived in Germany previously.

"Even though our ancestors were enemies, we can be friends," the other Turk said. The twins thanked them for the gift, and they remained friends all the time they worked together in that firm.

One of the jobs on which Steve served as project architect in this office was the Nassau Coliseum on Long Island. It is one of the largest covered stadiums for multi-purpose use in the United States. The coliseum's acoustics are excellent for operatic performances, and the sight lines are perfect, with no obstructions to the view from any seat, whether viewing hockey, basketball, or opera. In contrast, when New York's new Madison Square Garden opened in 1968, as many as 7,000 people, not able to see well enough from the seats in the rear, had to stand. It took several years to redesign and renovate to correct this problem.

Some years later, after Voya took a job with Kettering Medical Center in Kettering, Ohio, as director of the Architecture and Design Department, he proposed altering the national code by introducing a new classification in the *Guidelines for Construction and Equipment of Hospitals and Medical Facilities*. This classification would reduce sound transmission coefficient ratings for patient room access corridors for so-called composite walls, thus reducing construction costs. His proposal was unanimously accepted and published in the *Guidelines*.

It took time, effort, perseverance, and God's providence, but the twins made a new life for themselves in their adopted country. No longer locked within confining borders and laboring like cogs in the wheel of the state, they were free to dream, create, and achieve. But the education provided by the communist system served them well. It was, after all, the only thing they took with them when they escaped. The brothers had taken two very diverse paths, but like the gray falcon they found a way to fly away even when there was no way out.

EPILOGUE

In 1964, five years after their wedding, Ann and Voya had a son, George Ilya, named after his two grandfathers. He has a B.F.A. in painting and is working as a fine artist. Steve and Diana's marriage yielded three children—Daniel, Maria, and Johnny. Daniel earned a B.A. in psychology and married a girl from New York named Lisa. Maria, with a M.S.W. degree, works as a social worker. She married a man who was also named Steve, and they have two daughters, Lindsay and Kelsey. Johnny earned a B.F.A. degree from the School of Visual Arts and works as principal and creative director for a marketing communications firm. He and his wife, Susan, have two sons, Jackson and Ethan. Mica and Nata's son Jovica, now called John, earned a M.M. degree in music and a B.A. in business and works in the financial sector. He is married to Faith.

Over the years Vera, the twins' younger sister, made several visits to see her family in the United States, but did not stay. She returned to her husband, Duja, in Šabac.

Their half-sister, Leka, never came to the United States, but her middle son, Pavle (PAHV-leh), the preacher, did. His wife and three children immigrated with him. He pastors an Adventist church in Florida. Pera, Leka's youngest son, successfully weathered the multiple expulsions from school for not attending Saturday classes and finally graduated as a medical doctor. It took him longer, but he is now employed by the current government as primarius doctor and is often seen on Serbian TV. He and Jova (YOH-va), Leka's eldest son, remain in Serbia.

Kaca and Djoka, whose wedding the twins attended in Paris, eventually left France and immigrated to Australia with his family. Years later Pastor Kanachky sponsored them as close relatives, and they resettled in America. Now the couple lives in Cleveland, Ohio. Djoka's brothers also immigrated to North America. Nikola lives in Stevensville, Michigan, and Pera lives in Kelowna, British Columbia, Canada.

Mladen and Mela and their five children (daughter Anica was born after the twins arrived in the United States) live in the Chicago area where Mladen runs a profitable family business.

The twins remain ever grateful for all that God has done for them, for the opportunities America has afforded, and for the freedom to worship as they choose. Many goodbyes have had to be said over the years. Voya's mother and three sisters have gone to their rest to await the resurrection. In the turbulent world in which we live today, their mother's theme rings ever clearer: *"Sve ce proci a Gospod ce doci* [Everything will pass and the Lord will come]." This remains the twins' eternal hope.

AN AMAZING STORY OF FAITH

This is the riveting true story of a teenage boy who found the courage to stand up and speak boldly about his God—in the Soviet army. Foolish? Maybe. Risky? Definitely. 978-0-8127-0457-0. Paperback, 128 pages.

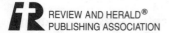

ANOTHER AMAZING STORY OF FAITH UNDER FIRE

Without warning, Mikhail Kulakov was arrested. His crime? Faithful service to God, or, in the words of the KGB, "anti-Soviet activities." Despite unrelenting persecution by his own country, he clung to God's promises. His unforgettable story will astonish, inspire, and humble you.
978-0-8280-2366-5.
Paperback, 192 pages.
US$15.99

AN UNBELIEVABLE STORY
OF GOD'S LEADING

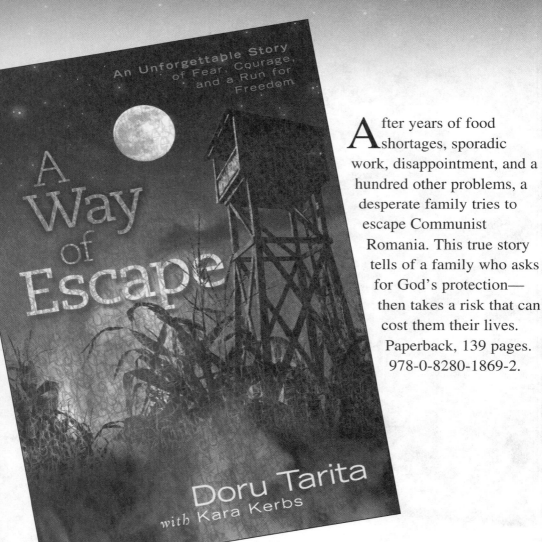

An Unforgettable Story of Fear, Courage, and a Run for Freedom

A Way of Escape

Doru Tarita
with Kara Kerbs

After years of food shortages, sporadic work, disappointment, and a hundred other problems, a desperate family tries to escape Communist Romania. This true story tells of a family who asks for God's protection— then takes a risk that can cost them their lives. Paperback, 139 pages. 978-0-8280-1869-2.

ANOTHER AMAZING STORY OF GOD'S LEADING

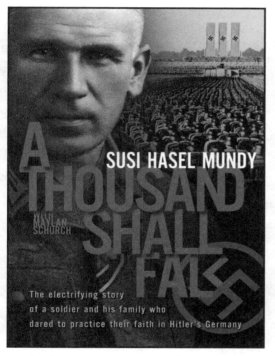

A Thousand Shall Fall

Susi Hasel Mundy

They saw God work miracle after miracle to save them from certain disaster. As thousands around them fell victim to the horrors of war, they were borne up on angels' wings—sometimes quite literally. This is the true story of one family who chose to be faithful whatever the cost. 0-8280-1561-9. Paperback, 172 pages.

3 WAYS TO SHOP

REVIEW AND HERALD®
PUBLISHING ASSOCIATION